WALT WHITMAN

Walt Whitman, 1841

Walt Whitman

REVISED EDITION

GAY WILSON ALLEN
New York University

DETROIT
WAYNE STATE UNIVERSITY PRESS
1969

811.3
W615 X
A425w

Published simultaneously in Canada by
The Copp Clark Publishing Company
517 Wellington Street, West
Toronto 2B, Canada

Reissued as Waynebook No. 31 (February, 1969)

Library of Congress Catalog Card Number 68-30926

Standard Book Number 8143 1380 9 (paper)
Standard Book Number 8143 1406 6 (cloth)

Cover: Walt Whitman, frontispiece, Leaves of Grass, *first edition,
from 1854 photograph*

137377

To

CHARLES E. FEINBERG

Distinguished Bibliophile and
International Benefactor of
Walt Whitman Scholars

Contents

SELECTED CRITICISM

☘ *Illustrations*

Picture Credits: New York Public Library, Oscar Lion Collection: cover, 20; Walt Whitman House, Camden: frontispiece, 1, 2, 3, 4, 6, 15; Brooklyn Museum: 7; New York Public Library, Stokes Collection: 8, 9, 12, 13; 14, 17; Museum of the City of New York: 10, 11; Museum of the City of New York, Clarence Davis Collection: 16, 18, 19; New York Public Library, Rare Book Room: 21; C. N. Elliott: 22, 61; Charles E. Feinberg: 23, 24, 40; Howell's *Literary Friends and Acquaintance:* 27; Drawing by Fred W. Oswald: 28; Photos by Mathew Brady 31, 37, 41, 67; *Harper's Weekly:* 32, 33, 34, 35, 36, 43, 45; U. S. National Archives: 37; Photo by Pearsall, Brooklyn: 42; Whitman Collection, Manuscript Division, Library of Congress: 47; Edward Naumburg, Jr.: 48; Missouri Historical Society: 51; Photo by Gutekunst, Philadelphia: 52; Milton I. D. Einstein: 54; Drawing by Charles Duhamel: 55; Photos by Walter W. Hollowell: 56, 57; Dr. William Reeder: 62; *Frank Leslie's Weekly:* 63; *Detroit Sunday Tribune:* 64, 65; University of Pennsylvania Library: 66; Pennsylvania Academy of the Fine Arts: 68.

 *Preface*

Though this illustrated book is intended primarily for the enjoyment of the non-specialist, I have tried to include something for anyone who is interested in Whitman. Even the scholar may find some of the pictures enlightening. I have given a rather full chronology, an almost complete checklist of the poet's publications, and selected biographical and critical titles.

My greatest indebtedness (excepting my wife, Evie Allison Allen) is to Mr. Charles E. Feinberg, who has generously furnished photographs and given permission for facsimile reproduction of the famous Emerson letter, as well as several Whitman holographs. Today no Whitman book could be written without the help of this greatest of all Whitman collectors, and this one least of all.

The staff of the New York Public Library has been extremely kind and efficient in tracking down and reproducing illustrations. Courteous assistance was also given by the Print Department of the Museum of the City of New York and the New York University Library at University Heights.

G. W. A.
Oradell, N.J.

Preface to Revised Edition

This life of Whitman in words (many of his own words) and pictures was written for the Evergreen Profile Series published by the Grove Press. Grove has since abandoned the Profile Series and this book has been out of print for several years. Even though my longer, more critical, biography *The Solitary Singer* has been republished by the New York University Press, letters to the author indicate that the Profile book is still needed and wanted. Since the Wayne State University Press is completely resetting and redesigning the book, I have had the opportunity to make some slight revisions, to overhaul the bibliographical check-lists, and to add a new section of selected criticism which gives some definite indications of the changes in critical attitudes toward Whitman from his death in 1892 to the present decade.

G. W. A.
March 15, 1968

Whitehead's comments on Whitman quoted by permission of the publisher from *Dialogues of Alfred North Whitehead* (Little, Brown and Company, 1954).

"Whitman's Innovations," reprinted from *The Young Rebel in American Literature: Seven Lectures*, ed. Carl Bode (London: William Heinemann Ltd., 1959), with permission of author and publisher.

"Some Lines from Whitman," by Randall Jarrell, reprinted by permission of the publisher from *Poetry and the Age* (Alfred A. Knopf, 1953).

"Symbols of Dimension," by Gay Wilson Allen and Charles T. Davis, quoted by permission of publisher from Introduction to *Walt Whitman's Poems. Selections with Critical Aids* (New York University Press, 1955).

WALT WHITMAN

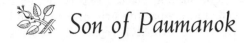 # Son of Paumanok

From Paumanok starting I fly like a bird,
Around and around to soar to sing the idea of all. . . .

GROWING UP ON LONG ISLAND

No American author better illustrates Taine's theory of the shaping influence of heredity, environment, and epoch than Walt Whitman. Not only was Whitman himself aware of these influences, he eagerly embraced them and adopted in his maturity the ambition to give poetic expression to his time, place, nation, and the development of his own character and talent in the midst and with the help of these forces. One biographer has remarked that Whitman's physical life was uneventful, that it was his rich inner life that mattered. Probably every great poet lives more intensely in his imagination than in his physical existence, but Whitman also lived through some of the most exciting and fateful epochs of American history. All of these he observed with perceptive interest, and in the Civil War hospitals he was more than a side-line spectator. His heredity, place of birth, and the time in which he lived are, therefore, of vital importance in understanding Whitman's life and work.

Whitman's poem, "Starting from Paumanok," romanticizes the facts, but it contains the kernel of biographical truth:

Starting from fish-shape Paumanok where I was born,
Well-begotten, and rais'd by a perfect mother,
After roaming many lands, lover of populous pavements,
Dweller in Mannahatta my city, or on southern savannas, . . .

The starting place, Long Island, or Paumanok as the Indians called it, is a narrow strip of land extending from the East River, separating Brooklyn from New York City, to Montauk Point, one hundred and twenty miles to the east. Its south shore is washed by the Atlantic Ocean, its north shore by the calmer water of Long Island Sound, which separates the Island from Connecticut and the southeastern tip of New York State. The early Dutch settlers of New Amsterdam spilled across the East River and gradually expanded over the western end of the island. In the seventeenth century English settlers arrived from Puritan Connecticut and established farms and villages around Huntington, toward the center of the Island where the land was most fertile and only a day's drive by horse-drawn vehicle from the markets in Brooklyn and New York.

Family tradition dated the arrival of the first Whitmans at Huntington around the middle of the seventeenth century, and legal records show this date to have been substantially correct. At one time the Whitman estates were extensive—as much as five hundred acres, according to this same family tradition, though the estimate cannot be verified by records; but they were greatly diminished during the two generations preceding the birth of the poet.

At first antagonistic to each other, the Dutch and English families gradually intermarried, while the Indians retreated farther toward the stony, wind-swept eastern tip of the Island. Farming remained the chief occupation of the inhabitants, though some became merchants, carpenters, fishermen, and sailors as towns rose and population grew. In its mixed nationalities and its predominantly rural inhabitants Long Island was a miniature of the rising nation. During the American Revolution most of the Islanders, including the Whitmans, supported independence. The poet's father, Walter Whitman, inheritor of this fierce patriotism, named three of his sons for national heroes: George Washington, Thomas Jefferson, and Andrew Jackson.

Walter Whitman married Louisa Van Velsor, the daughter of a farmer and horse-breeder at nearby Cold Springs Harbor, a jolly Dutchman called "Major" by his neighbors. But on her mother's side Mrs. Whitman was descended from Welsh seafaring men. Both the Van Velsors and the Whitmans lived close to the soil, but also near the sea. All loved to visit the shore: to cut marsh hay, to fish or dig for clams, to participate in sociable clambakes, and sometimes to sail away in ships. Some of the harbors were headquarters for whaling expeditions, and most of them were used in coast-wise shipping to points extending from Maine to Florida and the Caribbean.

In Whitman's own words, "Out from these arrières of persons and scenes, I was born May 31, 1819." That was only a few years after the War of 1812 with Great Britain, which gave a powerful boost to American confidence. The place was a little farming community called West Hills, near Huntington. Walt (christened Walter) was the second child of Louisa and Walter Whitman. Eventually Mrs. Whitman bore nine children, one of whom died in infancy. The father was a carpenter, who experienced great difficulty in feeding and clothing his growing family. As the years passed he moved many times, to Brooklyn when Walt was four, then back to various places on the Island, and again to Brooklyn, where he died in 1855.

Some biographers have doubted that Walt was "well-begotten and rais'd by a perfect mother." Certainly both parents were uneducated, and several of their offspring were plagued with physical afflictions that may or may not have been inherited. But there can be no doubt that Walt himself did inherit physical stamina, and from his mother a gentle, sympathetic disposition. His father seems to have been stern and taciturn, and it was not until middle age that Walt could remember him with sympathy. Most biographers believe that the poet described his own parents in the peom "There Was a Child Went Forth":

> *The mother at home quietly placing the dishes on the supper table,*
> *The mother with mild words, clean her cap and gown, a wholesome odor falling off her person and clothes as she walks by,*

*The father, strong, self-sufficient, manly, mean, anger'd,
    unjust,
The blow, the quick loud word, the tight bargain, the
    crafty lure,
The family usages, the language, the company, the furni-
    ture, the yearning and swelling heart,*

. . . .

*These became part of that child who went forth every day,
    and who now goes forth, and will always go forth
    every day.*

During his childhood Walt lived in two worlds, Brooklyn, a
thriving port competing with big New York City, and rural
Long Island. He liked to watch the busy harbor, to ride back
and forth on the ferries connecting the two cities, and he easily
made friends with longshoremen, fishermen, and the pilots of the
ferries. But it was also fun to ride back to Cold Springs Harbor
with his grandfather on the wagon in which "Major" Van Velsor
had brought fruit, vegetables, and other farm products to the
city markets. Little Walt loved every foot of the Island, and
in his old age he found great pleasure in recalling the scenes and
activities of his youth. In *Specimen Days*, for example:

> Worth fully and particularly investigating indeed this
> Paumanok, (to give the spot its aboriginal name), stretching
> east through Kings, Queens and Suffolk counties, 120 miles
> altogether—on the north Long Island sound, a beautiful,
> varied and picturesque series of inlets, "necks" and sea-like
> expansions, for a hundred miles to Orient point. On the
> ocean side the great south bay dotted with countless hum-
> mocks, mostly small, some quite large, occasionally long
> bars of sand out two hundred rods to a mile-and-a-half from
> the shore. While now and then, as at Rockaway and far
> east along the Hamptons, the beach makes right on the
> island, the sea dashing up without intervention. Several
> light-houses on the shores east; a long history of wrecks,
> tragedies, some even of late years. As a youngster I was in
> the atmosphere and traditions of many of these wrecks, of
> one or two almost an observer. Off Hempstead beach for

example, was the loss of the ship "Mexico" in 1840, (alluded to in "the Sleepers" in L. of G.). And at Hampton, some years later, the destruction of the brig "Elizabeth," a fearful affair, in one of the worst winter gales, where Margaret Fuller went down, with her husband and child.

Inside the outer bars or beach this south bay is everywhere comparatively shallow; of cold winters all thick ice on the surface. As a boy I often went forth with a chum or two, on those frozen fields, with handsled, axe and eel-spear, after messes of eels. We would cut holes in the ice, sometimes striking quite an eel-bonanza, and filling our baskets with great fat, sweet, white-meated fellows. The scenes, the ice, drawing the hand-sled, cutting holes, spearing the eels, etc., were of course just such fun as is dearest to boyhood. The shores of this bay, winter and summer, and my doings there in early life, are woven all through L. of G. One sport I was very fond of was to go on a bay-party in summer to gather sea-gull's eggs. (The gulls lay two or three eggs, more than half the size of a hen's eggs, right on the sand, and leave the sun's heat to hatch them.)

He also knew the eastern end, the Peconic Bay region. "I used to like to go down there and fraternize with the blue-fishers, or the annual squads of sea-bass takers. Sometimes, along Montauk peninsula (it is some 15 miles long, and good grazing), met the strange, unkempt, half-barbarous herdsmen, at that time living there entirely aloof from society or civilization, in charge on those rich pasturages, of vast droves of horses, kine or sheep, own'd by farmers of the eastern towns. Sometimes, too, the few remaining Indians, or half-breeds, at that period left on Montauk peninsula, but now I believe altogether extinct." (He was wrong about the latter, for some of them still live near Montauk.)

As he wrote about these experiences, "the soothing rustle of the waves" and "the saline smell" came back to him. He remembered also that in later years "while living in Brooklyn, (1936–1850) I went regularly every week in the mild seasons down to Coney Island, at that time a long, bare unfrequented shore, which I had all to myself, and where I loved, after bathing,

to race up and down the hard sand, and declaim Homer or
Shakespeare to the surf and sea-gulls by the hour."

In Brooklyn Walt attended public school for about six years,
but his reminiscences provide few details. We can guess that the
contemporary educational methods of rote memory and rigid
discipline did not endear school to him and there are many indications that he was an indifferent student. The experiences of
these years which he later described were only indirectly related
to school. In his fifth year General Lafayette came to Brooklyn
to lay a cornerstone for a library and by chance, as Whitman
liked to recall in old age, lifted him into a safe position during the
ceremony. In his tenth year the steam frigate Fulton blew up in
the nearby Brooklyn Navy Yard, killing forty-three sailors. Walt
heard the blast while at school, and later attended the military
funeral, being much impressed by the muffled drums and solemn
dead march. In the same year he went with his parents to hear
the Quaker schismatic, Elias Hicks, preach in a hotel because
churches were closed to him.

This reminiscence throws some light on the parents as well as
the schoolboy. Walt's father was not a member of any church
and seldom attended religious services. He had been a personal
friend of Tom Paine, the notorious "freethinker," and was probably a freethinker himself. The old man who had aided American
independence during the most discouraging days of the Revolution lived out his years in poverty and infamy (the result of
his publishing *The Age of Reason*) in Brooklyn, and there Walter
Whitman knew and befriended him before marrying and settling
at West Hills.

During Walt's youth Paine was one of his father's heroes. And
the socialists Frances Wright and Robert Dale Owen, somewhat
inclined toward "freethinking" too, were others. Elias Hicks, a
very devout man but independent in his theology, was a long-
standing friend of the Whitman family, from Walt's grandfather
Whitman (who died before Walt was born) to his own parents.
Mrs. Whitman's mother had also been a Quaker, but she herself

did not regularly attend any church until near the end of her husband's life, when she joined the Baptist church. But she was always ready to go with her husband to hear Elias Hicks preach, and at least once Walt accompanied them. The sincerity and fervor of the old man, who would not take off his Quaker hat to any man, even wearing it in the pulpit, so impressed Walt, that he became one of the poet's own special heroes. The numerous references in *Leaves of Grass* to Quaker customs owe more to Elias Hicks himself than to devotion to the Quaker church.

During his public school years Walt attended Sunday school at St. Ann's Episcopal Church, unaccompanied by his parents. Even in old age he remembered St. Ann's with tenderness, but he was never a churchgoer after childhood. Nevertheless, his mother's sympathy for religion and his childhood experiences in Sunday school no doubt influenced his adult reverence for religion, which he thought—and intended—to permeate *Leaves of Grass*.

The Whitman family moved frequently during Walt's youth, but usually toward the less settled part of Brooklyn, where land was cheapest. His father worked faithfully at his carpenter's trade, but found it difficult to support his growing family on a carpenter's wages. He tried speculating in real estate with little success; he simply had no head for business. It was necessary, therefore, for the boys of the family to become self-supporting at an early age. Walt's older brother, Jesse, went to sea. At the age of twelve or thirteen Walt himself began working as an office boy, first for a doctor and then for a law firm composed of a father and son. The father, Edward C. Clarke, Whitman recalled, "kindly help'd me at my handwriting and composition, and, (the signal event of my life up to that time), subscribed for me to a big circulating library." This was the real beginning of the boy's education and preparation for future authorship. Without losing interest in his outings on Long Island, Walt became a great reader, especially of novels. Later he discovered the New York theaters and continued his self-education in literature and art.

PRINTER, TEACHER, JOURNALIST

Before his fourteenth year Walt began an apprenticeship in printing. He was taught by an old patriot named William Hartshorne, who had lived in Philadelphia while the nation's capital was located there. Walt never tired of hearing Mr. Hartshorne tell patriotic stories about Washington. But learning to set type was a more disciplined education. Standing on old type cases to enable him to reach all the letters in the typebox, holding the "stick" awkwardly in his left hand, he learned to spell the words as he slowly, letter by letter, inserted them in lines of type. At that time most writers overpunctuated, and Walt Whitman never unlearned the customs of punctuation he acquired in the printing office. But acquiring the *feel* of a word, a sentence, or a paragraph is good training for any writer. Like Benjamin Franklin before him, and William Dean Howells and Mark Twain after, he learned to write less with pen and ink than with the alphabet of the type cases.

The owner of the shop in which Walt set type was also the editor of a newspaper, the *Long Island Patriot,* and he permitted the young apprentice to contribute "sentimental bits" to the paper. Seeing his own words in print gave Walt confidence a few years later to contribute anonymously to George P. Morris's "then celebrated and fashionable *Mirror* of New York City." He would always remember his emotions on receiving the magazine, "opening and cutting the leaves with trembling fingers," and how "it made my heart double-beat to see my *piece* on the pretty white paper, in nice type." In such manner is the vanity of authorship born!

By 1835 Walt had completed his apprenticeship and was employed in New York City as a printer. But two disastrous fires in that year brought an economic depression, and in 1836 he began to teach country schools on Long Island. By this time the Whitman family had moved back to the country, and for a while Walter, Sr. attempted to farm, apparently with no more success than in his other ventures. Walt refused to do farm work, and he and his father quarreled. Mrs. Whitman, always the "peacemaker," soothed the ruffled emotions of the son and father.

In spite of his own meager formal education, Walt Whitman had some important qualifications for teaching, at a time when few were required by school boards. He loved children, and they usually responded to his affection, including his own younger brothers and sisters. Unlike most teachers of the period, he believed in keeping discipline by persuasion rather than the rod. He strove constantly to find ways to interest the children in the tasks he set for them. He played "Twenty Questions" with them and invented other educational games.

The school terms were short, usually not over three months; the salary averaged $35 to $40 and board for a term; and the hours and duties were long and exhausting. The fact that Whitman taught in nearly a dozen schools between the summer of 1836 and the spring of 1841 is no reflection on him, but a revealing indication of the shortness of the terms and the instability of the teaching profession at that time.

Teaching did not prevent Whitman from writing and publishing a considerable number of sentimental poems and stories. One of the stories describes a young man greatly resembling the author who began teaching in discontent, after failure in New York as a result of the great fire, but whose "spirits were eventually raised and sweetened by his country life, by his long walks over the hills, by his rides on horseback every Saturday." Years later Whitman called his teaching "one of my best experiences and deepest lessons in human nature."

At the time, however, he continued to write imitative poems in the "graveyard" tradition. One of these began:

> *O mighty powers of Destiny!*
> *When from this coil of flesh I'm free—*
> *When through my second life I rove,*
> *Let me but find one heart to love*
> *As I would wish to love.*

The loneliness and melancholy in these trite poems may have had some basis in the frustrated ambition and emotional instability of the young schoolmaster, but even more certainly they testify to his intellectual immaturity. They show not the slightest spark of the bold originality, soaring imagination, and powerful imagery of *Leaves of Grass*. In old age the poet correctly said they came from the top of his mind.

Despite the satisfaction he found in teaching, Whitman felt that he should make use of his knowledge of printing and journalism. Consequently, in the spring of 1838 he started a weekly newspaper in Huntington, which he named the *Long Islander*. This is his own account of the venture: "I went to New York, bought a press and types, hired some little help, but did most of the work myself, including the press-work. Everything seem'd turning out well (only my own restlessness prevented me gradually establishing a permanent property there), I bought a good horse, and every week went all round the country serving my papers, devoting one day and night to it. I never had happier jaunts—going over to south side, to Babylon, down the south road, across to Smithtown and Comac, and back home. The experiences of those jaunts, the dear old-fashion'd farmers and their wives, the stops by the hayfields, the hospitality, nice dinners, occasional evenings, the girls, the rides through the brush, come up in my memory to this day."

The young man's restlessness caused him to sell his business, dispose of Nina, his horse, which he said was the saddest part of it, and try his luck once more in New York City. But there his luck had not changed, and he was forced to return to the Island for two more years. Once again he taught school, worked in a printing office at Jamaica, and electioneered for the Democratic candidate for the Presidency, Martin Van Buren, who was running in 1840 for a second term. Van Buren lost, and Whitman's efforts were wasted. It was a rough campaign, one of the most malicious in American history, and another ambitious young man named John Gunn, campaigning for the Whig candidate, William Henry Harrison, used dirty tactics, including lies and threats of physical violence, but Whitman defied him to the end. "From my very soul," he wrote in his party newspaper, the *Long Island Democrat*, "I look with sorrow on the pitiable and blacksouled malice which actuates such men as this young Gunn, who has lately been uttering the most reckless falsehoods, and endeavoring to stain, by mean and ungentlemanly misstatements, the standing of our most reputable citizens."

This is the language of a shocked idealist, and that is undoubtedly what Walt Whitman was in 1840. He was just beginning to learn the "ungentlemanly" tactics of politicians, and he still had a bitter education to complete in this unruly school.

1. Walt Whitman, early 1840s

2. Walt Whitman's birthplace, West Hills, Long Island

3 and 4. Walt Whitman's father and mother

5. *Walt Whitman's favorite sister Hannah (Mrs. Charles Heyde)*

6. *George Whitman, Civil War photograph*

7. *Brooklyn in 1816, painting by Francis Guy*

8. *Great Fire, New York, December 16, 1835*

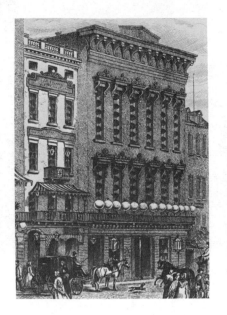

10. *Broadway Theatre, 1850s*   11. *First Bowery Theatre, 1826*

9. *New York, view from Brooklyn, c. 1840*

12. New Orleans, c. 1848

13. Brooklyn, view from New York, 1845

14. *Lower Broadway, New York, 1840s*

Habitant of Mannahatta

My city's fit and noble name resumed,
Choice aboriginal name, with marvelous beauty, . . .

PRINTER AND EDITOR IN NEW YORK

It was nearly two decades after Walt Whitman went to New York City in the spring of 1841 that he wrote a poem called "Mannahatta," using the "aboriginal name," but the city he described in the poem was the same "island sixteen miles long, solid-founded," lapped by

> *Tides swift and ample, well-loved by me, toward sundown,*
> *The flowing sea-currents, the little islands, larger*
> *adjoining islands, the heights, the villas,*
> *The countless masts, the white shore-steamers, the lighters,*
> *the ferry-boats, the black sea-steamers well model'd,*
> *The down-town streets, the jobbers' houses of business,*
> *the houses of business of the ship-merchants and*
> *money-brokers, the river-streets,*
> *Immigrants arriving, fifteen or twenty thousand in a*
> *week,*
> *The carts hauling goods, the manly race of drivers of*
> *horses, the brown-faced sailors,*
> *The summer air, the bright sun shining, and the sailing*
> *clouds aloft,*
> *The winter snows, the sleigh bells, the broken ice in the*
> *river, passing along up or down with the flood-tide*
> *or ebb-tide,*

The mechanics of the city, the masters, well-form'd,
    beautiful-faced, looking you straight in the eyes,
Trottoirs throng'd, vehicles, Broadway, the women, the
    shops and shows,
A million people—manners free and superb—open voices
    —hospitality—the most courageous and friendly
    young men,
City of hurried and sparkling waters! city of spires and
    masts!
City nested in bays! my city!

The young man from Long Island—"Paumanok"—felt at home in the great city, not only because he had visited it many times in his youth, crossing the East River by ferry hundreds of times, but also because it too was an island, and he had always loved the ocean, ships, and the crowded docks. In 1841, as in 1860, the life of New York depended upon the ocean, more than today, when much of its transport is carried by train or huge ships in the air. Furthermore, the city proper was then on the lower end of the island, near the Battery, and the busiest places were the wharfs along the Hudson below Thirty-fourth Street, or on the east side opposite Brooklyn. Herman Melville, a contemporary inhabitant of Manhattan, commented in *Moby-Dick* on the fascination of the water for all New Yorkers:

> There now is your insular city of the Manhattoes, belted round by wharves as Indian isles by coral reefs—commerce surrounds it with her surf. Right and left, the streets take you waterward. Its extreme down-town is the battery, where that noble mole is washed by waves, and cooled by breezes, which a few hours previous were out of sight of land. Look at the crowds of water-gazers there.

On a dreary Sunday afternoon, Melville continues, every one heads for the water: "Nothing will content them but the extremest limit of the land; loitering under the shady lee of yonder warehouse will not suffice. No. They must get just as nigh the water as they possibly can without falling in. And there they stand—miles of them—leagues. Inlanders, all, they come from lanes and alleys, streets, and avenues—north, east, south, and west. Yet here they all unite. Tell me, does the magnetic virtue of the needles of the compasses of all those ships attract them thither?"

That Whitman was one of the most fascinated of these "water-gazers," he himself confesses time and again. His first employment in the spring of 1841 was as a printer for the *New World*, which maintained one of the largest printing offices in the city, near Printing House Square. He boarded on lower Manhattan, and one of his favorite walks was in Battery Park.

In the spring of 1842, two months before his twenty-third birthday, Whitman became editor of a lively daily newspaper called the *Aurora*. Although he held this position for only about two months, his editorials give us vivid impressions of the life of the city, and his private enjoyment of his strolls down Broadway to the Battery, dressed in the latest fashion, carrying "a heavy, dark, beautifully polished, hook-ended" cane. He especially enjoyed the afternoon crowds on Broadway when women of fashion paraded their finery, the noisy firemen dashing to a fire, the roar of the busy markets, but above all the sight of the ships circling the island with a forest of masts and tanned sailors from all parts of the world embarking or disembarking or celebrating shore leave in the shooting galleries, saloons, and low dives in the Bowery.

Whitman took it all in, and based much of his "copy" for the printer on his observations and diversions. But he also took great satisfaction from his new responsibilities and confidence in the performances of his duties. On March 29, 1842, he confided:

> Without vanity, we can say that the *Aurora* is by far the best newspaper in the town. It is bound to no party, but fearless, open and frank in its tone—brilliant and sound, pointed without laboring after effect, ardent without fanaticism, humorous without coarseness, intellectual without affectation—and altogether presents the most entertaining melange of the latest news, miscellaneous literature, fashionable intelligence, hits at the times, pictures of life as it

is, and everything else that can please and instruct—far
beyond any publication in the United States. Its chief editor,
and his coadjutors, are among the ablest writers of America;
and each one "knows his part, and does it well."

Two weeks later he boasted:

> Every day that passes over our heads, encourages us
> more and more in our determination to render *Aurora* the
> paper of the city. Though we do not expect to set the North
> river on fire, we are free to confess, without vanity, that we
> have full confidence in our capacities to make *Aurora* the
> most readable journal in the republic. We are hourly ac-
> costed in the streets, in hotels, in places of mercantile resort,
> every where, with compliments, and praises of the boldness,
> beauty, and merit of our paper.

One should remember that this exuberant editor was not quite
twenty-three, and that in many respects he was fulfilling his
boastful ambitions. At any rate, the *Aurora* under his editorship
did give many interesting "pictures of life" as it was in New York
in 1842. For example, this was a period of many reform movements: prohibition (the owners of the *Aurora* also published the
Washingtonian, official paper of an anti-alcohol society), health
fads, abolition of slavery, women's rights, socialism, free love,
mesmerism, religious cults, and new philosophies. On March 7
Whitman printed an account of a lecture given by Ralph Waldo
Emerson in New York:

> The Transcendentalists had a very full house on Saturday
> evening. There were a few beautiful maids—but more ugly
> women, mostly blue stockings [intellectuals]; several in-
> teresting men with Byron collars, doctors, and parsons;
> Grahamites [Graham bread health cult] and abolitionists;
> sage editors, a few of whom were taking notes; and all the
> other species of literati. Horace Greeley was in ecstacies
> whenever any thing particularly good was said, which
> seemed to be once in about five minutes—he would flounce
> about like a fish out of water, or a tickled girl—look around,

to see those behind him and at his side; all of which very plainly told to those both far and near, that he knew a thing or two more about these matters than other men.

This lecture was on the "Poetry of the Times." He [Emerson] said that the first man who called another an ass was a poet. Because the business of the poet is expression —the giving utterance to the emotions and sentiments of the soul; and metaphors. But it would do the lecturer great injustice to attempt anything like a sketch of his ideas. Suffice it to say, the lecture was one of the richest and most beautiful compositions, both for its matter and style, we have ever heard anywhere, at any time.

Of course this report tells us very little about Emerson or his lecture, and one detects the superficiality of the writer, but it is hardly surprising that Whitman was superficial at this stage of his life. He did take an active interest in politics and social agitations of the day, often lambasting Tammany for cowardice or hypocrisy, criticizing the demagoguery of the "Native American" movement though he himself was strongly nationalistic, and opposing the use of state funds for supporting parochial schools. Irish immigrants were pouring into the city, most of them without funds or skills to make them readily employable, and clashes between the Irish and "Nativists" gangs were frequent, sometimes developing into serious riots which greatly alarmed Whitman. His editorials plainly reveal the social tensions and dilemmas of life in New York in the 1840's. It would perhaps be asking too much of so inexperienced an editor to expect him to offer objective analyses and practicable solutions. Those he left for Horace Greeley in the *Tribune*, James Gordon Bennett in the *Herald*, and William Cullen Bryant in the *Post*.

Whitman was in his natural element in describing his walks and loitering, in which he may have engaged too freely. This, in fact, was the charge made by his employers, with whom he quarreled around the end of April. On May 3 the *Aurora* carried this jibe: "There is a man about our office so lazy that it takes two men to open his jaws when he speaks." The quarrel may have been over policy, and the charge of laziness only an excuse, but whatever the cause, Walt Whitman was out of a job.

During the summer of 1842 he edited another paper in New York called the *Evening Tattler*, and Whitman used its pages to prolong his quarrel with the owners of the *Aurora*. This was an age of personal journalism and vitriolic feuds in print were common, sometimes resulting in duels and physical violence. Even dignified William Cullen Bryant horsewhipped an opponent on the street. Perhaps Whitman's apparent laziness averted a similar episode, for certainly many of his editorials were provocative.

FREE-LANCING AND POTBOILING

While editor of the *Aurora* and the *Tattler*, and later in the year when he may have been unemployed for a few months, Whitman was steadily turning out stories and a few poems— evidence that his laziness was more apparent than real—for popular magazines. Between January and September, 1842, the *Democratic Review* printed five of his stories, with sentimental, melancholy titles like "Tomb Blossoms," "A Legend of Life and Love," and "The Angel of Tears." More ambitious was his propaganda novel, *Franklin Evans, or the Inebriate*, which was printed in an extra of the *New World* (on which he had set type the previous year) and sold at 12½ cents a single copy. It was a melodramatic tale of a country boy who went to New York, became a drunkard, and eventually caused the death of three women who loved him. He was, of course, finally redeemed and the novel given a pious ending. In later years Whitman was so ashamed of this potboiler that he claimed to have written it in the reading room of Tammany Hall, while fortifying himself with gin cocktails. But the truth is that in 1842 he seriously believed in prohibition, a cause which he continued to advocate for several years.

Although in 1842 Whitman held no one position for more than two or three months, this was undoubtedly the most varied and exciting year he had experienced up to that time. During the next two and a half years he held other editorial positions, did a great amount of hackwork, and continued to turn out mediocre but salable stories. One of the most interesting was "Richard Parker's Widow," published in the *Aristidean* April, 1845. Richard Parker was the leader of the mutiny in the British Navy which Herman Melville half a century later used as the setting of his masterpiece, *Billy Budd*. Though no masterpiece, Whitman's fictionizing of the widow's loyalty to her martyred husband is vividly and effectively told. However, fiction was not Whitman's natural literary medium, and he soon gave it up.

Some time in August, 1845, weary of trying to earn a precarious living in New York, Whitman returned to Brooklyn for a new period of journalistic experience in the city where he had spent most of his life and to which his parents had recently returned after a discouraging attempt to make a living in the country on Long Island.

He certainly returned home by ferry, and perhaps at floodtide and sunset, which he later so beautifully described in "Crossing Brooklyn Ferry." With his back to "mast-hemm'd Manhattan," he "Look'd on the haze on the hills southward and southwestward," toward the "beautiful hills of Brooklyn," while the sea gulls oscillated overhead and the summer sky shimmered in the undulating water below.

East River Recrossed

I too many and many a time cross'd the river of old, . . .

EDITOR IN BROOKLYN

All of his life Walt Whitman would continue to admire and revisit New York City, but his professional life ended there in August, 1845. Whatever regrets he may have had at the time, it was not difficult for him to find consolation on Long Island in August. His sister Mary was married to a mechanic, Ansel Van Nostrand in Greenport, once a whaling port but now a summer resort. Walt always enjoyed visiting her there, where good country food and bluefish, his favorite, were plentiful. His younger brother, Jeff, now twelve, also liked fishing and boating, and sometimes they would go as far as Peconic Bay, on the east end of Long Island. There is no record of where they went in the summer of 1845, but this would have been a good time for such a trip, before Jeff became a printer's apprentice (a short time later he began studying surveying) and Walt assumed new duties.

Walt's father was having difficulty, as usual, in supporting his family. He worked hard as a carpenter, and had begun to build and sell houses on a speculative basis. But he had never been and never would be a successful business man. The houses were always mortgaged and he seldom made any money on his deals. Fortunately some of his children were beginning to be self-supporting. His oldest daughter was married, as mentioned above. Hannah, two years younger, was still at home, though now fully grown at twenty-two. Jesse, his oldest son, had gone to sea. Andrew worked irregularly. George, now sixteen, was beginning to earn money at odd jobs, sometimes as a carpenter's helper.

In September Walt was employed on the *Long Island Star*, a small daily newspaper owned and operated by old Alden J. Spooner, whom the Whitman family had known for many years. Mr. Spooner, a Whig, did not trust his young Democratic employee to write on politics. Consequently Walt turned to local subjects, such as the schools in Brooklyn, which he knew from firsthand experience, as a student and as a teacher in similar though smaller schools. The first of his stories to be published in the *Democratic Review* (1841) had been a gruesome tale, "Death in a School-Room," about a sickly boy flogged to death by a brutal schoolmaster. Now he had a chance to present his view on this subject more effectively to the public—at least more in detail, and in a newspaper that the teachers themselves would read. Most teachers in Brooklyn still believed in corporal punishment, and some of them showed their resentment of his articles by writing protests. These convinced Whitman more strongly than ever that educational reform was needed. After attending a lecture by Horace Mann in Brooklyn, he reported the great educator as saying, "They who expel wrong doing by means of physical chastisement cast out devils through Beelzebub, the prince of devils." Whitman asked rhetorically, "Are not some of our Brooklyn teachers a little too profuse of this satanic power?"

But these articles for the *Star* were not exclusively concerned with this subject, or even with schools. Whitman reported amateur theatrical performances—usually sarcastically—and music programs, many of the better ones in New York City, from whose entertainment he had not cut himself off just because he was now living in Brooklyn. Also he frequently gave moral and practical advice to young people, for he was more of a "columnist" (to use a modern term) than an ordinary reporter.

On February 26, 1846, the editor of the rival newspaper, the

Brooklyn Eagle, died, and Whitman was chosen to take his place. Although only five years old, the *Eagle* had already out-grown the *Star.* Moreover, it was Democratic, and now Whitman could be as partisan as he wished—or, more accurately, as he had been employed to be. He was now twenty-seven, and less brash than he had been on the *Aurora,* but just as resolute—or stub-born—as his employer, Isaac Van Anden, local Democratic "boss," was to learn.

The spring of 1846 was as exciting a period as any the nation had known since the War of 1812. The dispute with Great Britain over the Oregon Territory was coming to a head. Fremont was blazing a new trail to California, which the United States was an-nexing to prevent its being seized by Great Britain, Russia, or some other foreign power. And Texas, unilaterally annexed the previous year, had now to be defended by military force. After settling cautiously into his editorial duties, Whitman took up all these causes with the most ardent patriotism, seasoned with the highest idealism. On June 6 he shouted: "We pant to see our country and its rule far-reaching, only inasmuch as it will take off the shackles that prevent men the even chance of being happy and good—as most governments are now so constituted that the tendency is very much to other way ... [But] the mere physical grandeur of this Republic ... is only desirable as an aid to reach the truer good, the good of the whole body of the people."

Whitman honestly believed his own country to be, as he stated in an editorial on June 23, "ages ahead" in the struggle for free-dom. He even compared the American faith in democratic rule to "the faith which the Christian has in God's mystery." For the moment he seemed to forget that slavery existed in a part of his nation, though he had always detested this Southern institution. Before the year was out, however, he had become greatly alarmed over the efforts of Southern politicians and their sympa-thizers to extend slavery into the annexed territories. And he became even more alarmed over the possibility that the dispute might break up the Union. On February 6, 1847, he anticipated Lincoln by this editorial statement: "If there is a political bless-

ing on earth, that deserves to stand in the near neighborhood of
the great common blessings vouchsafed us by God—life, light,
freedom, and the beautiful and useful ordinations of nature—
that blessing is involved in the UNION of these United States
. . . and integral Republic, 'many in one.' "

Thereafter he was relentless in his fight for "free soil," partly
because he saw the extension of slavery as a threat to free laboring
men; partly because he believed that those vast, fertile lands of
the West must be saved as a refuge for the "masses of the
down-trodden of Europe," to enable them to achieve that destiny
"which we may suppose God intends for mankind."

His stand on "free soil" was Whitman's political undoing. In
1847 the Democratic Party split on a bill introduced into Congress
by Representative David Wilmot, prohibiting slavery in annexed
territories. Whitman hammered away in his editorials at all Democrats who did not support the Wilmot Proviso. But Van Anden
was one of the local leaders of the opposition to it, and he dis-
charged his unmanageable editor in January, 1848.

NEW ORLEANS INTERLUDE

Other newspaper editors of the region printed rumors that
friends of the recent editor of the *Eagle* were raising funds to
start a new "free soil" paper with him in charge, but the rumored
assistance was slow in materializing and Whitman had become impatient. While attending a performance at the Broadway Theatre
in New York, he met between acts a man from New Orleans, J.
E. McClure, who was planning soon to start, with his partner,
A. H. Hayes, a newspaper in New Orleans. As Whitman later
recalled, "after fifteen minutes' talk (and a drink) we made a
formal bargain and he paid me two hundred dollars down to bind
the contract and bear my expenses to New Orleans."

The first issue of the paper, to be called the *New Orleans
Crescent*, was to appear on March 5. At that time a trip from
New York to New Orleans was an exhausting journey by train,
stagecoach, and steamboat, taking two weeks or more; conse-

quently, two days later Whitman, accompanied by his young brother Jeff, set out by train for Baltimore. There they transferred to another train that carried them to Cumberland, Maryland, where they changed to a stagecoach for a bumpy trip across the Allegheny Mountains.

At Wheeling, West Virginia, they boarded a steamboat, which took them by Louisville, Cincinnati, and on to Cairo, Illinois, where the Ohio River flows into the Mississippi, and thence to New Orleans. The boat also carried freight of almost every description, from groceries, dry goods, hardware, to live hogs, fowls, and horses. It was an education in American life for Whitman, who had never before been farther away from home than the eastern tip of Long Island. They arrived at their destination on February 25.

New Orleans was exciting, almost like a foreign city with its French-speaking Creoles, French and Spanish architecture, tropical flowers, an impressive Catholic cathedral, a cemetery below sea level, a waterfront almost as busy as the Brooklyn docks, and American soldiers and officers passing through the city on their way home after service in the recent war with Mexico. One evening at the theater Whitman was thrilled to see General Zachary Taylor, whom he had praised without stint in *Brooklyn Eagle* editorials. The hero of Buena Vista had entered unnoticed while the lights were low, but between scenes he was recognized and the orchestra played "The Star Spangled Banner," followed by "Hail Columbia."

But New Orleans was also disappointing, for it was low, humid, and smelly, and Jeff was afflicted almost continuously by dysentery. His work in the newspaper office was too heavy for him—lifting sacks of mail—and he was dreadfully homesick. At first Walt enjoyed his work on the paper, and he wrote a number of character sketches with some of the same exuberance he had shown in his articles for the *Aurora*. But in less than three months after joining the *Crescent* he found the owners of the paper unfriendly—he was never quite sure why—and he resigned.

Walt and his brother Jeff left New Orleans on May 27, returning home by way of the Mississippi, the Great Lakes, and the Hudson River. The boat trip to Chicago was slow, wearing, and unpleasant. The boat was crowded, Jeff was ill, and the first night Walt had to sleep on the floor. But from Chicago on Walt enjoyed the trip, especially his exploratory strolls in Milwaukee, Cleveland, and Buffalo. In a little notebook he carried with him he recorded this condensed record of the last part of the trip:

> We arrived in Buffalo on Monday evening [June 12, 1848], spent that night and a portion of the next day in examining the place. In the morning of the next day, got in the cars and went out to Niagara. Great God! what a sight! We went under the Falls, saw the whirlpool, and all the other things, including the suspension bridge.
> On Tuesday evening we started for Albany and travelled all night. From the time daylight afforded us a view of the country, found it very rich and well cultivated. Every few miles there were large towns and villages.
> On Wednesday evening we arrived in Albany. Spent the evening in loitering about; there was a political meeting (Hunker) at the capitol [this was the faction that had deprived him of his editorship of the *Eagle*], but we passed it by.
> Next morning started down the Hudson in the *Alida*. Never before did I look upon such grand and varied scenery. Arrived about 5 o'clock in Brooklyn. Found all well.

The return trip had taken nineteen days.

WOUNDED IN THE HOUSE OF FRIENDS

This long journey through parts of the nation that Whitman had previously only heard, read, and dreamed about was almost sufficient compensation for his disappointment in the New Orleans position. Furthermore he arrived in Brooklyn just when the political cauldron was about to boil over again. During the summer of 1848 both political parties held conventions and nominated candidates for the Presidential election to be held in No-

vember. The Democrats nominated General Cass, arch-opponent
of the Wilmot Proviso. The Whigs nominated General Taylor and Millard Fillmore without taking any stand on the "free
soil" issue. As a result the anti-slavery men of both parties began
trying to organize a third party to be called Free Soil. Brooklyn
supporters of this movement appointed as delegates to a Free
Soil convention both Whitman and his former Whig employer,
Alden Spooner, who could not stomach Cass any more than
Whitman could now accept his former idol, General Taylor. At
the convention, held in Buffalo during August, Martin Van Buren
was nominated for President and Charles Francis Adams for Vice-
President.

Backers of this third party in Brooklyn also raised funds for a
Free Soil newspaper, and accepted Whitman as editor. He called
it the *Brooklyn Freeman,* and published the first issue on September 9. But on that very night his printing office was completely
destroyed by a fire that ravaged downtown Brooklyn, and he
was not able to resume publication of the *Freeman* until after
the election, in which the Free Soil Party made a poor showing
but drew enough votes away from the Democrats to cause their
defeat. During the winter of 1848–49 Whitman was able to ex-
pand the *Freeman* from a weekly paper to a daily paper. But the
Old Hunkers and Barnburners made peace, and with the Free
Soil Party in ruins and the Democrats of New York State once
more opposed to him, Whitman's support soon evaporated. He
managed to continue until September 11, 1849, when he published
the last issue and announced the end of the *Freeman.*

Not only was Walt Whitman once more unemployed, but he
was utterly disillusioned and disgusted with politics. His feelings
were too strong for adequate expression in prose and he once more
turned to poetry, this time savagely. He based one poem, which
the *New York Tribune* published on June 14, 1850, on the
Biblical text (Zechariah xiii, 6), "I was wounded in the house of
my friends." In a verse form suggesting blank verse, but actually
nearer free verse, he poured sarcastic taunts on the Northern be-
trayers of freedom:

> *If thou art balked, O Freedom*
> *The victory is not to thy manlier foes;*
> *From the house of friends comes the death stab.*
>
> *Vaunters of the Free*
> *Why do you strain your lungs off southward?*
> *Why be going to Alabama?*
> *Sweep first your own door;*
> *Stop this squalling and this scorn*
> *Over the mote there in the distance;*
> *Look well to your own eye, Massachusetts—*
> *Yours, New York and Pennsylvania;*
> *—I would say yours too, Michigan,*
> *But all the salve, all the surgery*
> *Of the great wide world were powerless there.*
> . . . .
>
> *Hot-headed Carolina,*
> *Well may you curl your lip;*
> *With all your bondsmen, bless the destiny*
> *Which brings you no such breed as this.*
>
> *Arise, young North!*
> *Our elder blood flows in the veins of cowards—*
> *The gray-haired sneak, the blanched poltroon.*
> *The feigned or real shiverer at tongues*
> *That nursing babes need hardly cry the less for—*
> *Are they to be our tokens always?*
>
> *Fight on, band braver than warriors,*
> *Faithful and few as Spartans;*
> *But fear not most the angriest, loudest, malice—*
> *Fear most the still forked fang*
> *That starts from the grass at your feet.*

Not even in this angry and pessimistic protest is Whitman giving up to despair, for he ends by saying that the fewer the warriors, the braver they must be. Exactly a week later (June 21, 1850) another poem of his was printed in the *Tribune* in which he asserted more positively that he did not despair of Liberty. It bore the awkward title of "Resurgemus," meaning the re-

surgence of hope that the revolts against tyranny in Europe in
1848 brought to all lovers of freedom and equality:

> *Suddenly, out of its stale and drowsy air, the air of slaves,*
> *Like lightning Europe le'pt forth,*
> *Sombre, superb and terrible,*
> *As Ahimoth, brother of Death.*
> . . . .
> *Liberty, let others despair of thee,*
> *But I will never despair of thee:*
> *Is the house shut? Is the master away?*
> *Nevertheless, be ready, be not weary of watching,*
> *He will surely return; his messengers come anon.*

It seems very unlikely that a man with Whitman's journalistic
experience and wide acquaintance with editors could not obtain
another newspaper position. Greeley accepted these poems for
the *Tribune,* and Bryant, the editor of the *New York Post,* was
a good friend of his, with whom he had often taken long walks.
Surely they could have helped him to obtain another position.
One must conclude that Walt Whitman did not want another
newspaper position. He did not want to risk further betrayal by
political compromisers. He was sick of the profession of journalism precisely because he believed so strongly in freedom and
justice for all humanity. He would earn a living somehow, but it
would be honestly obtained.

ART AND ARTISTS

Although Whitman had been interested in the theater since
his apprentice days and through the years had attended all the
theaters in New York City, his failure in journalism gave him
more time for this and other esthetic enjoyments. Around 1850
he also became intimately acquainted with a group of painters
and sculptors who had recently settled in Brooklyn. He already
knew William Sidney Mount, the Long Island portrait and genre
painter, and Walter Libby, a young man near his own age. But

it was in the studio of Henry Kirke Brown, who was to become famous for his bronze statue of George Washington (Union Square, New York City), that Whitman became acquainted with the cosmopolitan lives and opinions of contemporary artists: "Here I would meet all sorts—young fellows from abroad stopped here in their swoopings: they would tell us of students, studios, the teachers, they had just left in Paris, Rome, Florence."

One of Brown's young apprentices, John Quincy A. Ward, was to become more famous than his teacher. All were in revolt against the prudery and sentimentalism of contemporary American taste, which preferred the insipid Eves and Evangelines of Hiram Powers to the crude vigor of Ward's *Indian Hunter* (Central Park, New York City). During 1851–52 Horatio Greenough also wrote a series of articles in the *Democratic Review* defending the nude in art and preaching the need for a free, healthy, natural art in the United States. Like Whitman, he preferred "the roar of the Astor House" (New York's largest hotel) to the quiet of Trinity Church.

In February, 1851, Whitman wrote an article for the *New York Post* on an exhibition of paintings at the Brooklyn Art Union, and two months later he delivered a lecture on his own theory of art at this institution. His equation of "heroic action" and "sensitivity to moral beauty" was not startlingly original, but his speaking at the Union at all indicates the seriousness of his devotion to art, and his acceptance by artists.

For a decade Whitman had been attending performances of Italian opera, but the most brilliant period of opera in New York almost exactly coincided with his visits to Brown's studio. In 1851–52 he heard Bettini, Bosio, Badaili, Marini, and Steffanone, all famous stars, at the Astor Theater. About the same time he heard Bettini in Donizetti's *La Favorita* at Castle Garden, down at the Battery. There he also heard Jenny Lind, sensational "nightingale" imported from Sweden by P. T. Barnum; however, "The Swedish Swan, with all her blandishments, never touched my heart in the least."

It was during 1852–53 that the great soprano Marietta Alboni, then at the height of her power, came to America. Whitman heard her every time she performed, and was thrilled with "noble pleasure and happiness. . . . She used to sweep me away with whirlwinds." When the Academy of Music opened in 1854 on Fourteenth Street, Whitman attended the opera there, but no singer, in his opinion, ever equalled Alboni. Looking back on these years, he was convinced that, "But for the opera I could never have written *Leaves of Grass.*"

The World's Fair, with its famous Crystal Palace in imitation of the more renowned British Crystal Palace, which opened in New York on July 4, 1853, also contributed to Walt Whitman's education in art. As he recalled, "I went a long time (nearly a year)—days and nights—especially the latter—as it was finely lighted, and had a very large and copious exhibition gallery of paintings (shown at best at night, I tho't)—hundreds of pictures from Europe, many masterpieces—all an exhausting study—and, scatter'd thro' the building, sculptures, single figures or groups —among the rest, Thorwaldsen's *Apostles,* colossal in size—and very many fine bronzes, pieces of plate from English silversmiths, and curios from everywhere abroad—with woods from all lands of the earth—all sorts of fabrics and products and handiwork from the workers of the nations."

Of course Whitman's enjoyment of the Crystal Palace was not confined entirely to art. There he also enjoyed the companionship of other young men, especially the omnibus drivers, always his favorite companions, who had gone to this Exhibition mainly for amusement, which abounded in almost every variety. But it was intellectual curiosity that drew Whitman back time and again to the Egyptian Museum on lower Broadway. The collection had been assembled by Dr. Henry Abbott while practicing medicine in Cairo. Whitman had many long talks with Dr. Abbott concerning Egyptian antiquities "and what the old relics stand for, as near as we can now get." Later he wrote an article on this Museum for *Life Illustrated,* and scattered allusion and echoes of Egyptology through *Leaves of Grass.*

No one can say definitely how much these rich experiences in art studios, the opera, theaters, exhibits in the Egyptian Museum, and examining great paintings and sculptures at the World Fair contributed to the growth of *Leaves of Grass*, but they came exactly at the right time to stimulate and develop Whitman's esthetic sensibilities in the four or five years immediately preceding the printing of the first edition.

15. Walt Whitman, c. 1854

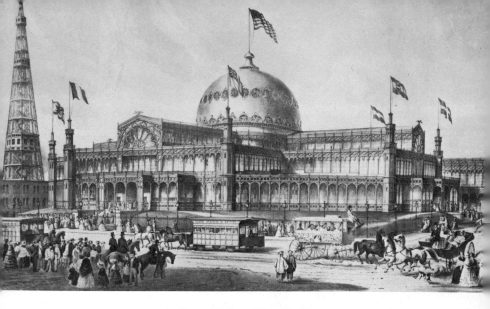

16. Crystal Palace, New York, 1853

17. Crystal Palace, interior, 1853

18. Castle Garden, New York, 1852

19. First appearance of Jenny Lind in America, Castle Garden, 1850

20. *Walt Whitman, frontispiece,* Leaves of Grass, *first edition*

22. *Ralph Waldo Emerson*

21. *Ornate binding,* Leaves of Grass, *first edition*

Walter Whitman, Esq.
Care of Fowlers & Wells.
308 Broadway.
New York.

Concord 21 July
Mass^tts } 1855

Dear Sir,

I am not
blind to the worth of
the wonderful gift of
"Leaves of Grass." I find
it the most extraordinary
piece of wit & wisdom
that America has yet
contributed. I am very

23 and 24. Letter to Whitman from Emerson, 1855

25. Title page, Leaves of Grass, *third edition, facsimile*

26. *Walt Whitman, frontispiece, Leaves of Grass, third edition*

27. *William Dean Howells and Walt Whitman, Pfaff's Restaurant, 1860*

28. *Calamus plant by F. W. Oswald*

CHANTS

DEMOCRATIC

AND

NATIVE AMERICAN.

O brood continental *(apostroph.)*

Apostroph.

O mater! O fils!
O brood continental! *name of the future* !
O flowers of the prairies!
O space boundless! O hum of mighty products!
O you teeming cities! Of so invincible, turbulent,
    proud!
O race of the future! O women!
O fathers! O you men of passion and the storm!
O native power only! O beauty!
O yourself! O God! O divine average!
O you bearded roughs! O bards! O all those slum-
    berers!
O arouse! the dawn-bird's throat sounds shrill! Do
    you not hear the cock crowing? *exultant*
O as I walk'd the beach, I heard the mournful notes
    foreboding a tempest—the low, oft-repeated
    shriek of the diver, the long-lived loon *I heard*

(105)

29. Page of Leaves of Grass, *third edition, facsimile*

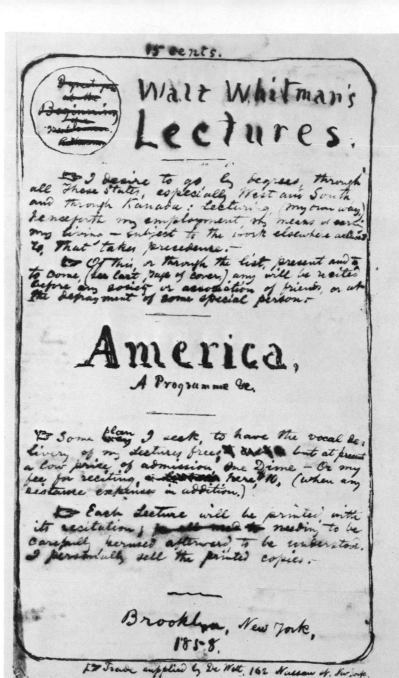

30. *Handbill planned by Whitman to announce his lectures, 1858*

What Is the Grass?

A child said What is the grass? fetching it to me with
  full hands, . . .
I guess it must be the flag of my disposition, out of
  hopeful green stuff woven.

BUSINESSMAN

Walt Whitman's first biographers, John Burroughs, William
Douglas O'Connor, and Dr. R. M. Bucke, fostered the myth that
between 1850 and 1855 he was a carpenter, and O'Connor did not
blush at suggesting a parallel with the Messiah carpenter of Gali-
lee. Whitman himself was guilty at least of letting this myth go
uncorrected. One of these biographers, Burroughs, may have
had some doubts, for he later wondered how a man so awkward
with tools as he observed Whitman to be could ever have earned
his living at carpentry.

It is now known, thanks to the indefatigable collecting of data
by Charles E. Feinberg (see bibliography), that Whitman never
supported himself on a carpenter's wages. His father, who was a
carpenter and unsuccessful speculator in real estate, began a
physical decline about the time Walt returned to Brooklyn from
New York (summer of 1845), and Walt gradually took over
the support of the family. Even the previous year he began to
buy real estate in Brooklyn, and by the time he edited the *Freeman* (1848–49) he was providing a house for the family to live
in and paying the bills.

The failure of the *Freeman*, therefore, made it urgently necessary for Whitman to find another means of income. First he tried operating a combined bookstore and printing shop on the first floor of the Whitman home, and from time to time he printed a "throwaway" advertising paper. Gradually his building activities increased until by 1852–53 he was making money, supporting his family adequately, and even buying such luxuries as a large old-fashioned Hall ["grandfather's"] clock, a melodeon, carpets, china, jewelry. It is unlikely that he was actually extravagant, but the purchases (for which Mr. Feinberg still has the receipts) are some indication of his business success. Though he frequently bought on credit, he was meticulously scrupulous in paying his bills. He was anything but the stock image of an impulsive, improvident poet.

Had Whitman continued in this way of life, he probably could have become, as he later asserted to friends, moderately wealthy. And he might have done so, had he not, early in 1855, become obsessed with a greater but less practical ambition. For several years he had been experimenting with a new poetic medium, and he had filled several notebooks with jottings and trial lines. A man of deliberate action, he did not rashly turn his back on business and rush into the role of poet. Perhaps at the time he did not intend to give up business, but only to postpone further building of houses for more urgent work—constructing a book of poems. Mr. Feinberg has neatly summed up the situation:

> Some biographers have treated Whitman as a careless idler, a drifter, a loafing dreamer, who never took his meals on time and worked only when he felt like it. What I have tried to say is that Whitman was a very practical young man, devoted to his family, making money to support them and being modestly successful in business matters. By 1855, he felt that he was ready to publish his *Leaves of Grass* and deliberately turned his back on all of his money making ventures, to do what he felt he was born to do, to be a writer, the poet and singer of America's songs, the architect of the American Dream.

ODD PUBLICATION OF A STRANGE BOOK

Myths have also grown up around the publication of Whitman's first *Leaves of Grass*. One is that he set the type with his own hands. Another is that it sold not a single copy—once while in a bitter mood in old age Whitman himself made this statement. Having been trained and employed for several years in the printer's trade, Whitman could, of course, have set the entire book himself, and he probably did set a few pages (once, trying to correct misstatements, he estimated that he actually set about ten pages). Unable to find a regular publisher for his manuscripts, he employed some friends of his known as the Rome brothers to print the book, though another firm had to take the printed sheets and bind them.

The binding was completed by the first of July, 1855, and the book was advertised on July 6 in the *New York Tribune*. This was the notice, printed, as was customary, on the first page:

WALT WHITMAN'S POEMS, "LEAVES OF GRASS," 1 vol. small quarto, $2, for sale by SWAYNE, No. 20 Fulton st., Brooklyn, and by FOWLER & WELLS, No. 308 Broadway, N. Y.

Four days later the name of Swayne was withdrawn from the notice, but Fowler & Wells continued to advertise the book for a month. Why Swayne withdrew is not definitely known, and distribution by Fowler & Wells is a little odd, too, for this was a firm of phrenologists. It is true that Mr. Lorenzo Fowler had previously examined the poet's cranium and pronounced him a genius, but *Leaves of Grass* was not phrenology, a pseudo-science as popular in the 1850's as psychoanalysis today. For a few years Whitman himself at least partly believed in it, yet to associate the 1855 *Leaves of Grass* in any way with phrenology is to misunderstand a book which seemed bizarre and shocking to most of the poet's contemporaries but today is almost universally accepted as one of the greatest masterpieces of nineteenth-century world literature.

Yet even the book was provokingly odd in appearance. It was a thin quarto of only ninety-five pages, bound in green cloth, ornately stamped with floral designs, the gold lettering of the title sprouting roots, leaves, and tentacles in all directions. The name of the author was not given on the title page, though it appeared in the copyright note. The frontispiece was an engraved photograph of a young man with a short beard, a Christ-like face, and wearing a dark, heavy felt hat cocked jauntily on his tilted head. Moreover, in an age of great dignity and formality in dress, this nonchalant poser with one hand in the pocket of his jeans and the other on hip, was in shirtsleeves, with collar open, showing the edge of a dark-colored undershirt, which the engraver later said was red flannel.

Withholding his name from the title page was not the result of modesty or a desire to remain anonymous. The frontispiece was intended by Whitman as a more personal way of announcing his authorship. Moreover, midway in his first, long, untitled poem (later called "Song of Myself") he announced himself very emphatically as

> *Walt Whitman, an American, one of the roughs, a kosmos,*
> *Disorderly fleshy and sensual . . . eating, drinking and*
>   *breeding,*
> *No sentimentalist . . . no stander above men and women*
>   *or apart from them . . . no more modest than immodest.*

An ambition which grew with Whitman in each successive edition of *Leaves of Grass* was to identify himself so closely with his book that the reader would have the illusion that the book was the man himself. As he later expressed it,

> *Camerado, this is no book,*
> *Who touches this touches a man, . . .*

This we may well call another myth about the first edition of *Leaves of Grass* (as well as the succeeding ones), that the man and the poet are identical, and that to know one is to know the other. It is doubtful that the artist and the man are ever identical, though the artist is a man (or a woman), and he may long to transform or rarefy his life into the perfection of art. But however much the artist may use his physical life as subject matter, the creation is always an alloy compounded of spirit and matter: experience sublimated, transformed by dream or wish-fulfillment, and shaped by esthetic intuitions. So it was with the first *Leaves of Grass*, for it was—and is—a work of art.

THE 1855 MANIFESTO

Internally the 1855 *Leaves of Grass* seemed even more eccentric to the poet's contemporaries than it did externally. The poems were preceded by a ten-page preface without a title, set double column in small type. Some of the paragraphs ran nearly two columns, and sentences defied conventional grammatical structure by continuing indefinitely through "and . . . and" or were broken like the caesura of an alexandrine by a series of periods. Actually this was a symbolical style, conveying a sense of space and continuity to the perceptive reader—of which Whitman had very few until many years later.

For several decades the demand in the United States for an indigenous art and literature had been growing louder. To some extent this was a patriotic reaction against England, and to a great extent the result of increasing national consciousness. One of Whitman's chief ambitions in 1855 was to answer the call for an American poet. Thus he announces in his preface, "here are the roughs and beards and space and ruggedness and nonchalance that the soul loves." The implication is plain that he intends to produce a literary art which shall have the strength, spaciousness, and confident indifference to precedent which will adequately represent or parallel nature's generosity to the United States—that is, generosity in natural resources and in nurturing a new breed of humanity, for such Americans believed themselves to be. This poet which Whitman describes and hopes to become shall be "commensurate" with the American people. "His spirit responds to his country's spirit . . . he incarnates its geography and natural life and rivers and lakes."

How can this "incarnation" be accomplished esthetically? Whitman does it by applying his metaphor spatially. When the nation expands physically (only ten years previously it had acquired vast new territories in Oregon, Texas, and California), he expands with it. To convey empathy of space, he enumerates, "on him rise solid growths that offset the growths of pine and cedar and hemlock and liveoak and locust and chestnut and cypress and hickory and limetree and cottonwood and tuliptree and cactus and wildvine and tamarind and persimon," and on through the flora and fauna and human activities of North America.

By enumerating substantives or concrete details, Whitman created a *montage* of images, a vast composite picture. But he was not, like Banvard, who painted a panoramic view of the Mississippi River on a canvas a mile long, trying to reproduce physical details with photographic realism. "The land and sea, the animals, fishes and birds, the sky of heaven and the orbs, the forests mountains and rivers, are not small themes . . . but folks expect of the poet to indicate more than the beauty and dignity which always attach to dumb real objects . . . they expect him to indicate the path between reality and their souls."

To Whitman the beauty, fecundity, and abundance of nature were, as he said later, in "Crossing Brooklyn Ferry," ministers to the soul. They symbolized spiritual truths. And poetry is a means of representing the meaning of these truths, by artistic techniques which are themselves organically symbolical: "the poetic quality is not marshalled in rhyme or uniformity or abstract addresses to things nor in melancholy complaints or good precepts, but is the life of these and much else and is in the ,soul. The profit of rhyme is that it drops seeds of a sweeter and more luxuriant rhyme, and of uniformity that it conveys itself into its own roots in the ground out of sight. The rhyme and uniformity of perfect poems show the free growth of metrical laws and bud from them as unerringly and loosely as lilacs or roses on a bush, and take shapes as compact as the shapes of chestnuts and oranges and melons and pears, and shed the perfume impalpable to form. The fluency and ornaments of the finest poems or music or orations or recitations are not independent but dependent. All beauty comes from beautiful blood and a beautiful brain. If the greatnesses are in conjunction in a man or woman it is enough. . . ."

Another aspect of this doctrine is Whitman's concept of *time*: "Past and future are not disjoined but joined. The greatest poet forms the consistence of what is to be from what has been and is. He drags the dead out of their coffins and stands them again on their feet . . . he says to the past, Rise and walk before me that I may realize you. He learns the lesson . . . he places himself where the future becomes present."

Notice that the poet "places himself where the future becomes present." In other words, by his imaginative revivification of the past and prophetic intuition of the future, he can not only show what ought to be, but actually bring it into being.

This was a romantic revival of one of the major beliefs of poets and artists of the European Renaissance: that the poet can profoundly affect human lives, and thereby even the destiny of nations. Thus Whitman asserts that the poets are "the voice and exposition of liberty." Their every action and gesture shall be an example. "The attitude of great poets is to cheer up slaves and horrify despots. The turn of their necks, the sound of their feet, the motions of their wrists, are full of hazard to the one and hope to the other. Come nigh them awhile and though they neither speak or advise you shall learn the faithful American lesson." The poet of all men is the one who is never discouraged by failure, for "Liberty is poorly served by men whose good intent is quelled from one failure or two failures or any number of failures, or from the casual indifference or ingratitude of the people. . . ." It is liberty above all that Whitman thinks important. "When liberty goes it is not the first to go nor the second or third to go . . . it waits for all the rest to go . . . it is the last."

Whitman's nationalism is easily misunderstood. By 1855 he had lost whatever jingoism he may have had as an editor in his youthful days; though even then he knew as well as anyone that complete liberty had not yet been achieved in the young self-styled "democratic" nation, for he had sacrificed position and newspaper career for "free soil." In this preface, therefore, he is an extoller not of accomplished fact but of ideal greatness. He wants to inspire Americans with their natural advantages and possibilities for greatness. Only when each man and woman realizes his innate, God-given potentialities will he be worthy of his nation and the nation of him." "An individual is as superb as a nation when he has the qualities which make a superb nation. The soul of the largest and wealthiest and proudest nation may well go half-way to meet that of its poets. The signs are effectual. There is no fear of mistake. If the one is true the other is true. The proof of a poet is that his country absorbs him as affectionately as he has absorbed it."

PHILOSOPHY OF THE SELF

The 1855 edition of *Leaves of Grass* contained twelve untitled poems, the first of which was later called "Walt Whitman," and finally "Song of Myself." Neither is an accurate title, for it is not the poet's own song of himself, but of *the* self. The poem says this in the opening lines:

> *I celebrate myself,*
> *And what I assume you shall assume,*
> *For every atom belonging to me as good belongs to you.*

As Thoreau remarks in defending his use of "I" in *Walden*, "I should not talk so much about myself if there were anybody else whom I know as well." The only *self* anyone knows is his own. But Whitman used himself as a bridge to selfhood. His real object is the nature of the self; its delight in being—and the joy of existence provides the lyrical emotion of the poem; the equality and perfection of all beings, the kinship and sacredness of all selves; the immortality of the soul, which is the metaphysical foundation of the self.

In a mystical intuition of the relation of body and soul, Whitman experiences "the peace and joy and knowledge that pass all the art and argument of the earth:

> *And I know that the hand of God is the elderhand of my*
> *   own,*
> *And I know that the spirit of God is the eldest brother of*
> *   my own,*
> *And that all the men ever born are also my brothers . . . and*
> *   the women my sisters and lovers,*
> *And that a kelson of the creation is love;*
> *And limitless are leaves stiff or drooping in the fields,*
> *And brown ants in the little wells beneath them,*
> *And mossy scabs of the wormfence, and heaped stones, and*
> *   elder and mullen and pokeweed.*

The poet does not say with Isaiah that "All flesh is grass," but he might have used this metaphor as his text, for not only does he believe all life—vegetables, animal, and spirit—to be related, but he also sees the grass growing out of graves, both physically and symbolically as a promise of rebirth of the self:

> *And now it seems to me the beautiful uncut hair of graves.*
> . . . .
>
> *This grass is very dark to be from the white heads of old*
> *   mothers,*
> *Darker than the colorless beards of old men,*
> *Dark to come from under the faint red roofs of mouths.*
>
> *O I perceive after all so many uttering tongues!*
> *And I perceive they do not come from the roofs of mouths*
> *   for nothing.*
>
> *I wish I could translate the hints about the dead young men*
> *   and women,*
> *And the hints about old men and mothers, and the offspring*
> *   taken soon out of their laps.*
>
> *What do you think has become of the young and old men?*
> *And what do you think has become of the women and*
> *   children?*

They are alive and well somewhere;
The smallest sprout shows there is really no death,
And if ever there was it led forward life, and does not wait
*   at the end to arrest it,*
And ceased the moment life appeared.

The "I" or *self* of this poem is itself a soaring spirit, wandering symbolically through time and space. First over the North American continent, sharing in the varied life and achievements of the people from ocean to ocean and from Canadian border to Southern limits. Like a god the poet "walks with the tender and growing night" and makes love to it:

Press close barebosomed night! Press close magnetic nour-
*   ishing night!*
Night of south winds! Night of the large few stars!
Still nodding night! Mad naked summer night!

Hovering in the sky, he looks down upon his beloved world swimming in space:

Smile O voluptuous coolbreathed earth!
Earth of the slumbering and liquid trees!
Earth of departed sunset! Earth of the mountains misty-
*   topt!*
Earth of the vitreous pour of the full moon just tinged with
*   blue!*
Earth of shine and dark mottling the tide of the river!
Earth of the limpid gray of clouds brighter and clearer for
*   my sake!*
Far-swooping elbowed earth! Rich apple-blossomed earth!
Smile, for your lover comes!

The poet's voluptuous love-affair with his physical world makes him truly a cosmic poet. His strongest and most vivid images evoke cosmic connotations:

To behold the daybreak!
The little light fades the immense and diaphanous shadows,
The air tastes good to my palate.

*Hefts of the moving world at innocent gambols, silently
    rising, freshly exuding,
Scooting obliquely high and low.*

*Something I cannot see puts upward libidinous prongs,
Seas of bright juice suffuse heaven.*

He has "instant conductors" which "seize every object and
lead it harmlessly through one." Every "touch" is sexual, "quivering me to a new identity." The perpetuity of life is a cosmic prin-
ciple; the climax of sexual touch is

*Parting tracked by arriving . . . perpetual payment of the
    perpetual loan,
Rich showering rain, and recompense richer afterward.*

*Sprouts take and accumulate . . . stand by the curb prolific
    and vital,
Landscapes projected masculine full-sized and golden.*

Santayana has called this poet a barbarian wallowing in his
own sensibilia. And so it would be if we did not see the larger
context, which is to say the symbolism of the poet's sensuality,
the kinship he feels with all forms of life. In the animals he sees
"tokens" of himself, which he must have dropped as he "passed
that way untold times ago." Two years before the publication
of Darwin's *Origin of Species*, Whitman visualized the long
journey of the forms of life from the first faint germ in the
"foetid carbon" through the "bunches of ages" until he arrived
with his soul on the spot.

*Cycles ferried my cradle, rowing and rowing like cheerful
    boatmen;
For room to me stars kept aside in their own rings,
They sent influences to look after what was to hold me.*

*Before I was born out of my mother generations guided me,
My embryo has never been torpid . . . nothing could
    overlay it;
For it the nebula cohered to an orb . . . the long slow strata
    piled to rest it on . . . vast vegetables gave it sustenance,*

> *Monstrous sauroids transported it in their mouths and*
> *deposited it with care.*
>
> *All forces have been steadily employed to complete and*
> *delight me,*
> *Now I stand on this spot with my soul.*

On the historical level, Whitman identifies with his contemporaries, especially with all who suffer,

> *I do not ask the wounded person how he feels . . . I myself*
> *become the wounded person, . . .*

But his most lyrical identifications are with the cosmic and life-forces. Vicariously he soars in space until his "elbows rest in sea-gaps" and his "palms cover continents." Yet far or near, looking down at the grass or up at the stars, he is reminded of the "perpetual transfers and promotions" of the soul in its endless journey. This, finally, is the meaning of *self:* a link in the great chain of life. Like a speeding comet, the poet departs "as air," shaking his "white locks at the runaway sun," effusing his "flesh in eddies" and drifting it in "lacy jags." Yet paradoxically,

> *I bequeath myself to the dirt to grow from the grass I love,*
> *If you want me again look for me under your bootsoles.*

The other poems in the first edition (except for the inclusion of the earlier verse treatment of the 1848 revolutions in Europe and a satire on the arrest in Boston of the runaway slave Anthony Burns) merely extend or reiterate the themes and motifs in the first poem. The third, later called "To Think of Time," treats, with an undertone of irony, the self-importance and fear of death that make it so difficult for human beings to think of their not existing.

> *To think that the rivers will come to flow, and the snow*
> *fall, and fruits ripen . . . and act upon others as upon*
> *us now . . . yet not act upon us;*
> *To think of all these wonders of city and country . . . and*
> *others taking great interest in them . . . and we taking*
> *small interest in them.*

The main purpose of this poem is the same as that of Lucre-
tius in *De Rerum Natura*, to combat the fear of death.

> *Do you suspect death? If I were to suspect death I should*
>   *die now,*
> *Do you think I could walk pleasantly and well-suited to-*
>   *ward annihilation?*
> . . . .
> *I swear I see now that everything has an eternal soul!*
> *The trees have, rooted in the ground . . . the weeds of the*
>   *sea have . . . the animals.*

If Walt Whitman has a major theme, this is it, in 1855 and
later. The fourth poem in the first edition, later called "The
Sleepers," most beautifully symbolizes the poet's faith in the
natural cycles of life, death, and rebirth.

> *I will stop only a time with the night . . . and rise betimes.*
>
> *I will duly pass the day O my mother and duly return to*
>   *you;*
> *Not you will yield forth the dawn again more surely than*
>   *you will yield forth me again,*
> *Not the womb yields the babe in its time more surely than*
>   *I shall be yielded from you in my time.*

Whitman was the "poet of democracy" in the sense that he
shared completely the American faith in the sacredness of the
self and the American dream of its fullest development. His major
symbols, however, were of death and rebirth: grass, graves,
cradles, "journeywork of the stars," night and dawn. But he was
not in love with death, as some critics have asserted. His faith in
the purposes of death intensified his ecstatic enjoyment of the
life of the senses.

Fame in Concord

One world is aware and by far the largest to me, and that
is myself,
And whether I come to my own to-day or in ten thousand
or ten million years,
I can cheerfully take it now, or with equal cheerfulness I
can wait.

GREETING FROM EMERSON

The indifference of poets to fame is a familiar paradox in the history of literature. Of all artists they most need an audience, and rare indeed is the poet who does not openly or secretly long for recognition, though many protect their pride by feigned indifference. Whitman ended his 1855 preface with a test which he undoubtedly hoped to meet: "The proof of a poet is that this country absorbs him as affectionately as he has absorbed it." However long he could "cheerfully wait"—and it was to be long, and not always cheerful—he did not neglect practical steps. Of the less than eight hundred copies printed and bound of the first *Leaves of Grass*, he sent out several dozen review copies to magazine and newspaper editors in the United States and Great Britain, and complimentary copies to prominent authors.

Most authors either ignored the book, or like Whittier threw it into the fire. But one copy that found its mark was the one addressed to Ralph Waldo Emerson, perhaps more famous as a lecturer than as a poet, but in 1855 nevertheless one of the most admired and respected literary men in the United States. The philosophy expressed or implied by Whitman in his poems closely resembled Emerson's own Transcendentalism (though derived in part from Carlyle, one of the sources for American Transcendentalism). It is not surprising, therefore, that Emerson should see merit in the book. But the spontaneity and warmth of his approval was remarkable. This has been called, with good reason, the most famous letter in the history of American letters. Though it has been quoted many times (often from a slightly inaccurate copy made by Whitman himself), it is worth quoting again.

> Concord 21 July
> Massts.   1855

Dear Sir,

   I am not blind to the worth of the wonderful gift of "Leaves of Grass." I find it the most extraordinary piece of wit and wisdom that America has yet contributed. I am very happy in reading it, as great power makes us happy. It meets the demand I am always making of what seemed the sterile & stingy nature, as if too much handiwork or too much lymph in the temperament were making our western wits fat & mean. I give you joy of your free & brave thought. I have great joy in it. I find incomparable things said incomparably well, as they must be. I find the courage of treatment, which so delights me, & which large perception only can inspire. I greet you at the beginning of a great career, which yet must have had a long foreground somewhere, for such a start. I rubbed my eyes a little to see if this sunbeam were no illusion; but the solid sense of the book is a sober certainty. It has the best merits, namely, of fortifying & encouraging.
   I did not know until I, last night, saw the book advertised in a newspaper, that I could trust the name as real & available for a postoffice. I wish to see my benefactor, & have felt much like striking my tasks, & visiting New York to pay you my respects.

> R. W. Emerson

Mr. Walter Whitman.

Any poet would have been thrilled by such a letter, especially from an older poet of Emerson's stature. Walt Whitman was electrified. After this even antagonistic reviews would not be able to dampen his ardor, and he was to receive many slashing attacks.

Not all reviews, however, were completely unfriendly. Charles A. Dana in the New York *Tribune* found the language of the poems "too frequently reckless and indecent," but declared them "certainly original in their external form"—i.e., versification. In *Putnam's Magazine* the book was called "a mixture of Yankee transcendentalism and New York rowdyism," though the anonymous reviewer, Charles Eliot Norton, praised it to some of his friends. Edward Everett Hale praised it publicly in the *North American Review*, and declared, in this very proper Boston magazine, that "there is not a word in it meant to attract readers by its grossness." It is a curious fact that conservative New England received the book much more sympathetically than sophisticated New York.

But evidently Whitman was not satisfied, for he wrote three anonymous reviews himself, possibly at the suggestion of editor-friends, and not as unusual a practice at that time as one might suppose. Then on the advice of Dana, Whitman later stated, he printed Emerson's letter in the *Tribune* (October 10, 1855) without first asking Emerson's permission. There were conflicting stories about Emerson's reaction, but however displeased he may have been, and probably was, he never retracted his endorsement. In fact, he visited Whitman in New York after his letter had been used to advertise *Leaves of Grass*. He took Whitman to dinner at a fashionable New York hotel, and afterwards Whitman took him to a social club for firemen, probably Firemen's Hall, on Mercer Street, completed in 1854 to the great pride and joy of New York fire-fighters.

On Emerson's recommendation other men visited Whitman, notably Henry D. Thoreau, whose *Walden* had been published with no great success the year before *Leaves of Grass*; Bronson Alcott, the unworldly educator and philosopher neighbor of Emerson; Frank Sanborn, abolitionist and another neighbor of Emerson; and Moncure D. Conway, a former Methodist minister, now an author of some consequence in the United States and England.

But it should not be assumed that Emerson was the only promoter of Whitman's fame. He was to learn later that the book had found favor with a small audience in both England and the United States. Some copies were sent to a British book dealer, who disposed of them finally through a peddler. It is impossible to estimate how many were sold in this country, but the best guess is between three and four hundred. The surprising fact is that so many of these have survived and are today in collections, both private and institutional. There were readers who appreciated and preserved a large number of copies.

It was not entirely Emerson's letter, therefore, that encouraged Whitman to prepare a second edition. This time the phrenological publishers, Fowler & Wells, backed it financially, though they did not risk announcing themselves as publishers. By late summer of 1856 the new edition had been printed from stereotype plates and was ready for distribution. It was a small, thick volume measuring four by six and a quarter inches, nearly 400 pages, bound in green cloth stamped with floral decorations similar to those of the first edition. On the backstrip in goldleaf letters were Emerson's words: "I Greet you at the Beginning of A Great Career." Inside Whitman printed the now famous letter, and an open letter reply addressed to his "Master."

This letter was boastful and did not show Whitman in one of his more admirable roles. But it set forth his ambitions of 1856, and he was right when he declared, "the work of my life is making poems." Few men in the history of literature have ever more courageously and tenaciously achieved such an ambition in the face of discouragement than did Walt Whitman. His first edition, he reminded Emerson, contained twelve poems. This one had thirty-two, including the original twelve. "I keep on till I make a hundred, and then several hundred—perhaps a thousand. The way is clear to me. A few years, and the average annual call for my Poems is ten or twenty thousand copies—more, quite likely."

Never in his lifetime would Whitman achieve anything close to such a sale, but from this time until his death he never stopped "making poems," and editing new, enlarged, and revised editions of *Leaves of Grass.* The growth of this book would henceforth be his life-work, the center of his intellectual life, the cause for which he would sacrifice himself without stint. Other poets have pursued their ambitions as single-mindedly, but Whitman's effort was unique in being devoted to *one* book—if the perennial *Leaves of Grass* can be called one book.

One theme which Whitman especially emphasized in the 1856 edition was sex; we might say a "sex program," for he announced in his letter to Emerson that "the body of a man or woman is so far quite unexpressed in poems," and he intended to celebrate "the eternal decency" of amativeness and motherhood. In "Poem of Women" the theme is maternity and self-reliance: "First the man is shaped in woman, he can then be shaped in himself." Another poem, though revised from the first edition, was called "Poem of Procreation." None of these was erotic, but of course they offended some readers because they asserted the importance of sex. In still another poem, with the odd title of "Bunch Poem," he called the phallus a poem, and described all nature as sexual, from the hairy bee that curves on "the full-grown lady-flower" to the "wet of the woods." The poet warned himself of "the meanness of me should I skulk or find myself indecent, while birds and animals never skulk or find themselves indecent."

> The oath of procreation I have sworn,
> The greed that eats in me day and night with hungry gnaw,
>   till I saturate what shall produce boys to fill my
>   place when I am through,
> The wholesome relief, repose, content . . .

Such sentiments continually shocked the prudish during the poet's lifetime.

But the second edition was not dominated by the sex program. Actually Whitman's intended role as the national poet began to emerge more clearly in this edition. In "Poem of Many in One" he saluted "A nation announcing itself," and himself announced

> *I myself make the only growth by which I can be*
> *appreciated,*
> *I reject none, accept all, reproduce all in my own forms.*

He even seemed to praise national isolationism,

> *America, curious toward foreign characters, stands sternly*
> *by its own,*
> *Stands removed, spacious, composite, sound . . .*

which he matched with his resolve to create his own literary and poetic standards and techniques. Here his cosmic inspiration was brought to bear on his program of matching the spirit of his country and its natural endowments. In "Poem of Salutation" (later "Salut au Monde") he asked, "What widens within you, Walt Whitman?" and found latitude widening, longitude lengthening. The "incarnation" program of 1855 was growing in the life and art of the poet. In the most impressive poem of the second edition, "Sun-Down Poem" ("Crossing Brooklyn Ferry"), he vicariously transcended time and place and felt at one with all who had already crossed the river by ferry or who would in the future do so:

> *I am with you, you men and women of a generation, or*
> *ever so many generations hence,*
> *I project myself, also I return—I am with you, and know*
> *how it is.*

The idea of defying the annihilation of time by creating a work of art was not original (see Shakespeare's sonnets, or Keats's "Ode on a Grecian Urn"), but Walt Whitman gave it a specific, vivid, American application in this, one of his finest poems. This alone was enough to insure him literary immortality.

"THE EIGHTEENTH PRESIDENCY"

The poet who hoped in 1856 that he was writing for posterity was acutely aware of the sorry plight of both political parties as the autumn Presidential elections approached. Franklin Pierce, elected in 1852, had made a weak President. The South had continued to dominate Congress, and in 1853 the pro-slavery Democrats had passed the Kansas-Nebraska bill, creating two new territories and declaring that the Compromise of 1850 (prohibiting the extension of slavery) did not apply to them, and Pierce had signed it. This resulted in violent skirmishes in Kansas, which was practically in a state of civil war while the political parties held their conventions in the summer of 1856. The Democrats nominated James Buchanan on a platform of "states rights" and "squatter sovereignty." The Know-Nothing or Native American Party nominated another nonentity, Millard Fillmore, and took no stand on slavery. Two years previously the Republican Party had been founded to oppose slavery, and it nominated John C. Frémont, Western explorer and colorful abolitionist.

As Whitman looked over the field of candidates, he felt little enthusiasm for any of them, but Frémont came nearest to his ideal. He wrote a political tract called "The Eighteenth Presidency," which ridiculed Buchanan and Fillmore and at least endorsed the kind of candidate that Frémont's supporters claimed him to be, though oddly enough, Whitman's description seems prophetic of the candidate four years later, Abraham Lincoln: "I would be much pleased to see some heroic, shrewd, full-informed, healthy-bodied, middle-aged, beard-faced American blacksmith or boatman come down from the West across the Alleghenies, and walk into the Presidency, dressed in a clean suit of working attire, and with the tan all over his face, breast, and arms; I would certainly vote for that sort of man, possessing the due requirements, before any other candidate."

Addressing directly the "Three Hundred and Five Thousand Owners of Slaves," Whitman declared in these prophetic words: "Suppose you get Kansas, do you think it would be ended? Suppose you and the politicians put Buchanan into the Eighteenth Presidency, or Fillmore into the Presidency, do you think it would be ended? I know nothing more desirable for those who contend against you than that you should get Kansas. Then would the melt begin in These States that would not cool till Kansas should be redeemed, as of course it would be . . . but not one square mile of continental territory shall henceforward be given to slavery, to slaves, or to the masters of slaves—not one square foot. If any laws are passed giving up such territory, those laws will be repealed . . . what laws are good enough for the American freeman must be good enough for you. . . ."

What use was made of this tract, no one knows. It survives in galley proofs, which Whitman apparently hoped would be copied and mass-distributed by some person or newspaper. So far as known, no one did. But the surviving proofs stand as evidence of Whitman's continued deep concern over the issues that had lost him the editorship of the *Eagle* and strangled the *Freeman*.

LAST NEWSPAPER EDITORSHIP

The only obvious result of "The Eighteenth Presidency" was that in the spring of 1857 the owner of the *Brooklyn Daily Times*, George C. Bennett, who supported the candidacy of Frémont for the Presidency in 1856, employed Walt Whitman to edit the *Times*. During the two years he edited this paper (it is difficult if not impossible to determine the exact terminal dates), Whitman let his poems lie fallow, giving all his attention to his newspaper duties, though he still found time for amusement in New York City.

In his editorials Whitman embraced such popular and democratic causes as running the street cars on Sunday for the benefit of laboring men on their one day of recreation, providing Brooklyn with pure, abundant water, and exposing political corruption on both sides of the East River. In May, 1857, he criticized the *New York Herald* for "croaking" a financial "crash," but when the predicted crash arrived in the autumn, he defended the soundness of the Williamsburg Savings Bank and helped prevent a "run" on the bank. This was characteristic of Whitman's civic-mindedness while editor of the *Times*. He denounced "Rowdyism," prize fights, and brutality and injustice of all kinds.

A characteristic and informative editorial was the one on vice published June 20, 1857:

> After dark, in the great City of New York, any man passing along Broadway, between Houston and Fulton streets, finds the western sidewalk full of prostitutes, jaunting up and down there, by ones, twos, or threes—on the lookout for customers. Many of these girls are quite handsome, have a good-hearted appearance and, in encouraging circumstances, might make respectable and happy women.

The editorial then describes their places and methods of housekeeping (Canal, Greenwich, Cherry, Water, and Walnut streets, and notorious Five Points), their clientele (sailors, canal-boatmen, country boys), the attendant drinking, quarreling, fighting, and so on. Then it continues on what is evidently a daring subject:

> Though of course not acknowledged or talked about, or even alluded to, in "respectable society," the plain truth is that nineteen out of twenty of the mass of American young men, who live in or visit the great cities, are more or less familiar with houses of prostitution and are customers of them . . . Especially the best classes of men under forty years of age, living in New York and Brooklyn, the mechanics, apprentices, seafaring men, drivers of horses, butchers, machinists, &c., &c., the custom is to go among prostitutes as an ordinary thing. Nothing is thought of it—or rather the wonder is, how there can be any "fun" without it.

The consequence is "the bad disorder," shame, concealment, degradation, completely ignored by "pious, orderly, fatherly persons":

> All these things go forward meanwhile, not permitted to be brought to light. In offices, in by places, hundreds of quacks are to-day dosing thousands of the best bodies in the land, with strong and never-erased drugs, mercury, bitter extracts, powerful salts and precipitates—exhausting the last dime of their victims . . .

If prostitution continues so, and the main classes of young men merge themselves more and more in it, as they appear to be doing, what will be the result? A generation hence, what a scrofulous growth of children! What dropsies, feebleness, premature deaths, suffering infancy to come!

This is not the voice of a Bohemian, though Whitman continued to dress in the unconventional manner affected in the frontispiece of his 1855 *Leaves of Grass*. A Brooklyn journalist has left us this description: "His dress was heavy, coarse, but clean, and seemed to belong to a farmer or a miner rather than to an editor . . . flannel trousers, belted and tucked into boots that reached to the knee, a peajacket never buttoned, a blue shirt open at the throat, a red kerchief at the neck, and a broad-brimmed hat! Even Horace Greeley, who affected a rustic make-up, was more conventional in his costume." Whitman no doubt dressed in this manner partly for economy, for there are evidences that he was very hard up at that time—and the depression of 1857 was a severe one—but it was symbolic too, and remained so throughout the rest of his life.

One of the contemporary events that most excited Whitman during his editorship of the *Times* was the laying of the Atlantic cable in 1858. When the first message was finally sent on August 17 (a greeting from Queen Victoria to the President of the United States), he joined all Brooklyn in the biggest celebration in the history of the city. Even repeated breaks and failures did not dampen his faith in the project, which was to become one of the motifs in a major poem, "Passage to India."

The language of the editorial on prostitution may give us a clue to the quarrels which Whitman is reputed to have had with Mr. Bennett over the conduct of the *Times*. He also criticized the churches for maintaining fire-traps, and very likely annoyed the pious and "respectable" readers of the paper. At any rate, his employment ceased some time in the summer of 1859, and, as usual, he turned once more to his poems. Had he succeeded as an editor, it is almost certain that the world would have lost a great poet; but he failed, and the world gained.

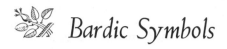 *Bardic Symbols*

I will make the song of companionship,
I will show what alone can compact These States, . . .

BOHEMIAN

On June 26, 1859, either just before or soon after Whitman lost his editorship of the *Times*, he wrote in his notebook: "It is now time to *stir* first for *Money* enough, to *live and provide for M---*. *To Stir*—first write stories and get out of this slough."

The "M" was in all likelihood an abbreviation for "Mother," but precisely what "slough" Whitman was in we do not know: financial, almost certainly; psychological, more than likely. He did not, so far as known, write any fiction at this time, but he did list himself in the city directory as "copyist," and he probably did some journalistic hackwork. His younger brother Jeff was now married, and this left Walt as the almost sole support of his mother and Eddie, for his older brothers Jesse and Andrew seem never to have assumed this responsibility. Hannah had also recently married an impecunious landscape painter, Charles Heyde, and moved to New England, from which she was soon sending back unhappy neurasthenic letters to her family in Brooklyn.

But in whatever way Walt supported his mother, he evidently had more leisure time than he had had on the *Times*, for this was the period of his frequent visits to Pfaff's Restaurant in New York City. Charles Pfaff, from German-speaking Switzerland, had established a restaurant in 1854 on Broadway, near Bleecker Street. By 1859 his wine and beer were regarded as the best in the City, and his basement bar had become the favorite "hangout" of a group of would-be Bohemian writers and artists. For two or three years Walt Whitman frequented it almost daily. One witness says that he was "the only one who was never tipsy and never 'broke' . . . he was an easy borrower, though it does not appear that he asked for large amounts or made needless delays in his repayments." Another witness, William Dean Howells, who came east in the summer of 1860 and sought out Whitman at Pfaff's, remembered "how he leaned back in his chair, and reached out his great hand to me, as if he were going to give it to me for good and all."

Bohemianism was not a native or natural institution in New York. But several habitués of Pfaff's had lived in Paris, and they were making a desperate effort to transplant the life and customs of the "left Bank" to New York. The leading self-styled Bohemian was Henry Clapp, editor of a spritely but unprofitable literary review called the *Saturday Press*. Another was Jane McElheney, better known by her pen name "Ada Clare," who had gone to Paris to bear the illegitimate child of Louis Moreau Gottschalk, leading pianist and composer of the United States. After her return she contributed to the *Saturday Press* and was called the "Queen of Bohemia." She and Whitman had become good friends. Adah Isaacs Menken, the notorious actress and later, reputedly, mistress to Swinburne, did not arrive until 1860. But Fitz-James O'Brien, Thomas Bailey Aldrich, E. C. Stedman, George Arnold, R. E. Stoddard, and William Winter were early members of the group—most of whom later became "respectable."

Henry Clapp encouraged Whitman and printed "A Child's Reminiscence" (later title: "Out of the Cradle Endlessly Rocking") in the special 1859 Christmas issue of the *Saturday Press*. This was to become the finest new poem in the third edition of *Leaves of Grass*.

"O SOLITARY ME"

"Out of the Cradle Endlessly Rocking," to use the final title, narrated tenderly and with deep pathos the story of a little boy on Long Island observing a pair of mocking birds (once common on the Island, ornithologists tell us).

> *Once Paumanok,*
> *When the lilac-scent was in the air and Fifth-month grass*
> *   was growing,*
> *Up this seashore in some briars,*
> *Two feather'd guests from Alabama, two together,*
> *And their nest, and four light-green eggs spotted with*
> *   brown,*
> *And every day the he-bird to and fro near at hand,*
> *And every day the she-bird crouch'd on her nest, silent*
> *   with bright eyes,*
> *And every day I, a curious boy, never too close, never*
> *   disturbing them,*
> *Cautiously peering, absorbing, translating.*

But one day the mother bird failed to return, "Nor ever appear'd again." All summer the little boy listened to the he-bird calling his mate, or so the boy believed. As he listened, he himself understood the meaning of love and death, and then he was no longer a boy but a poet in whom a thousand songs were starting to life.

> *O you singer solitary, singing by yourself, projecting me,*
> *O solitary me listening, never more shall I cease perpetuat-*
> *   ing you,*
> *Never more shall I escape, never more the reverberations,*
> *Never more the cries of unsatisfied love be absent from*
> *   me, . . .*

So far as known no records have survived either of an un-happy love-affair experienced by Whitman or the loss of a loved one by death in 1858 or 1859, but many of his manuscripts of this period testify to his sense of loneliness, solitude, and longing for love and friendship. Of course these moods were intensified by the loss of his editorial position and the failure of his second edition of *Leaves of Grass* to sell as he had anticipated it would in his boastful open letter to Emerson.

During September and October of 1859 Whitman's future seemed bleak indeed. A poem called "Bardic Symbols" (later title: "As I Ebb'd With the Ocean of Life"), which he published in the *Atlantic Monthly* the following spring after his luck had changed, records the poet's emotional and intellectual crisis. As he walked along the shore of Long Island late one autumn afternoon, he felt "seiz'd by the spirit that trails in the lines underfoot" and identified himself with the debris, with wreckage and failure.

> *I too but signify at the utmost a little wash'd-up drift,*
> *A few sands and dead leaves to gather,*
> *Gather, and merge myself as part of the sands and drift.*

This was no idle fancy, but a deep conviction of inadequacy and failure, almost of despair:

> *O baffled, balk'd, bent to the very earth,*
> *Oppress'd with myself that I have dared to open my mouth,*
> *Aware now that amid all that blab whose echoes recoil*
> *   upon me I have not once had the least idea who or what*
> *   I am,*
> *But that before all my arrogant poems the real Me stands*
> *   yet untouch'd, untold, altogether unreach'd,*
> *Withdrawn far, mocking me with mock-congratulatory*
> *   signs and bows,*
> *With peels of distant ironical laughter at every word I*
> *   have written,*
> *Pointing in silence to these songs, and then to the sands*
> *   beneath.*
>
> *I perceive I have not really understood any thing, not a*
> *   single object, and that no man ever can,*
> *Nature here in sight of the sea taking advantage of me to*
> *   dart upon me and sting me,*
> *Because I have dared to open my mouth to sing at all.*

But the frustration gave way to humility, and then to returning faith that "the flow will return," for such is the nature of both oceans, the physical one and the symbolical ocean of life.

THE TIDE TURNS

The "flow" did indeed return a few months later, suddenly and unexpectedly. During 1859 Whitman had his friends, the Rome brothers, set up a large number of new poems in order to provide him with copies in type which he hoped to use to attract a publisher of a new and enlarged edition of *Leaves of Grass*. His efforts to find a publisher were unsuccessful, but early in February, 1860, he received a letter from a young publishing firm in Boston, Thayer & Eldridge, offering to publish *Leaves of Grass*. The letter was written by the junior member of the firm, Charles W. Eldridge, who was henceforth to be one of the poet's most loyal friends. "When the book was first issued," Eldridge wrote, "we were clerks in the establishment we now own. We read the book with profit and pleasure. It *is* a true poem and writ by a *true* man."

A contract was quickly drawn up and on March 15 Whitman arrived in Boston to see his book through the press. He found a room in a cheap boarding house and settled down to revising his manuscripts and reading proof as they were set in type. Two days later Emerson came over from Concord, partly to welcome him and partly to protest the inclusion of poems on sex (to be called "Enfans d'Adam") in the forthcoming third edition. For two hours Emerson argued under the ancient elms of the Boston Common, but Whitman remained "more settled than ever to adhere to my own theory, and exemplify it." Emerson gave up gracefully, and both men "went and had a good dinner at the American House." Afterwards Emerson introduced him to the great Athenaeum library and secured reading privileges for him.

Emerson wanted to take Whitman to the famous Saturday Club, but Longfellow, Lowell, and Holmes insisted that they had no desire to meet him. Whitman's friends in Concord, Emerson,

Alcott, and Thoreau were also prevented by the women of their families from inviting him over as a house guest. This indicates the righteous prejudice that his first two editions had already created.

But Whitman made other friends in Boston, T. H. Bartlett, a sculptor; William Douglas O'Connor, author of an abolition novel called *Harrington;* Frank Sanborn, who was being tried for aiding a runaway slave; and John Townsend Trowbridge, journalist and novelist, who had read Dana's review of the first edition in the *New York Tribune* while in Paris and regarded it as "the most exhilarating piece of news from America during my six months of absence abroad." Hearing that Whitman was in Boston, Trowbridge searched him out and found "a gray-bearded, plainly dressed man reading proof-sheets at a desk in a little dingy office." One Sunday Trowbridge invited the poet to visit him at his home in Somerville, a suburb of Cambridge, and it was there that Whitman said that Italian opera and reading Emerson had been two of the greatest influences on his first *Leaves of Grass*.

Finally the book was printed and bound in May, and Whitman, homesick for Brooklyn and his friends at Pfaff's, was able to return. Henry Clapp did all he could in the pages of the *Saturday Press* to promote the sale of the book. He suggested that a review copy be sent to Mrs. Juliette H. Beach, one of his reviewers, but her husband seized the copy and sent in a savage review, which Clapp printed under the impression that Mrs. Beach had written it. Afterwards Mrs. Beach denied the authorship and tried to make amends by writing an anonymous defense strongly praising "the deep spiritual significance of Leaves of Grass." John Burroughs later claimed that Mrs. Beach wrote many beautiful letters to the poet.

It is a curious fact that a number of women came to Whitman's aid at this time. In the *Saturday Press* Mary A. Chilton of Islip, Long Island, defended the sex poems in this manner: "In childhood there is no blush of shame at sight of a nude form, and the serene wisdom of maturity covers this innocence with a halo of glory, by recognizing the divinity of humanity, and perceiving the unity of all the functions of the human body." Adah Menken wrote a eulogistic review too, and Ada Clare encouraged the poet personally. If Whitman did not have love affairs at this time, it was not for lack of opportunity; but his new poems show a deeper emotional attachment to men than women.

THE 1860 *LEAVES OF GRASS*

Some critics and biographers have called the 1860 edition of *Leaves of Grass* Whitman's most important and revealing version. Certainly it was, and still remains, one of his most interesting. It was a thick duodecimo volume of 546 pages, bound in heavy boards stamped with symbolical designs, on the front cover a globe swimming in space, on the back a sun half-risen (or half-set) out of the ocean, and on the backstrip a butterfly perched on an extended forefinger, evidently illustrating the cosmic, spatial, and nature themes and motifs of the book.

The frontispiece was an engraving made from an oil portrait of Whitman painted by his New York friend, Charles Hine. The bust showed the poet in an arty Victor Hugo pose, with curly hair, short beard, a Byronic collar, and dark silk scarf loosely knotted in a huge bow knot—almost an exact antithesis of the shirtsleeved, arms akimbo portrait of the first edition.

The book opened with a long prefatory poem called "Proto-Leaf" (later title: "Starting from Paumanok"), which had already been much revised (as manuscripts reveal), and still bore evidence of a bifurcation in the poet's ambition. It began autobiographically:

> *Free, fresh, savage,*
> *Fluent, luxuriant, self-content, fond of persons and places,*
> *Fond of fish-shape Paumanok, where I was born,*
> *Fond of the sea—lusty-begotten and various,*
> *Boy of the Mannahatta, the city of ships, my city, . . .*

And proceeded to the treatment of two themes, the poet's intention to "make a song for These States" and at the same time the propagation of the "ideal of manly love."

> *I will therefore let flame from me the burning fires that*
> *were threatening to consume me,*
> *I will lift what has too long kept down those smouldering*
> *fires,*
> *I will give them complete abandonment,*
> *I will write the evangel-poem of comrades and of love,*
> *(For who but I should understand love, with all its sorrow*
> *and joy?*
> *And who but I should be the poet of comrades?)*

These national and amatory motives the poet attempted to fuse
and reconcile by the doctrine that only personal love and companionship can "compact" These States.

This program is still a subject of keen debate among the Whitman critics, but at least the poet was consistent in organizing the
third edition around the two themes. In a group of poems called
"Chants Democratic" (some new, some revised from the 1855
and 1856 editions), Whitman attempted to advance his program
of literary nationalism, amplifying and applying the ideas first
announced in the 1855 preface:

> *These States are the amplest poem,*
> . . . .
>
> *By great bards only can series of people and States be*
> *fused into the compact organism of one nation.*
> . . . .
> *Underneath all is Nativity,*
> . . . .
> *The Many in One—what is it finally except myself?*
> *These States—what are they except myself?*

The group which was to become the most notorious was called
"Enfans d'Adam" (in later editions, "Children of Adam"). It
opened with this sonnet-like, free-verse poem:

> *To the garden, the world, anew ascending,*
> *Potent mates, daughters, sons, preluding,*
> *The love, the life of their bodies, meaning and being,*
> *Curious, here behold my resurrection, after slumber,*

The revolving cycles, in their wide sweep, having brought
    me again,
Amorous, mature—all beautiful to me—all wondrous,
My limbs, and the quivering fire that ever plays through
    them, for reasons, most wondrous;
Existing, I peer and penetrate still,
Content with the present—content with the past,
By my side, or back of me, Eve following,
Or in front, and I following her just the same.

The poetic inversion in the first line of this poem can be easily misread: its meaning is that the world must ascend once more to the Garden of Eden; not only recapture the lost innocence of Adam and Eve before their "fall," but also recover man's original strength and fecundity. This was both a rationalization of Whitman's doctrine of the goodness and purity of all natural physiological functions, including the sexual, and at the same time a part of the national myth, the American dream, which he shared: Here in the new world, with its unexhausted and unperverted natural resources man could achieve a new Eden on earth. Europe —so the myth held—was old, exhausted, diseased; America, young, innocent, and strong, could make a new start, establish new moral, ethical, social, and political standards.

Whitman believed that the poet—such as he dreamed of being —could formulate and propagate these new, needed concepts and ideals. Thus he, too, would beget a new generation on mothers (receptive acolytes) fit for conception. He intended his language to shock the prudish into a saner sexual tolerance, but more basically he was a cultural "begetter."

The same paradox of theme, imagery, and symbolism ran throughout the succeeding group of poems called "Calamus." For his major symbol Whitman used the phallic-shaped plant, calamus, or sweet flag, growing in swamps and bogs on Long Island and other damp places in the Eastern United States. Originally (as his notes and manuscripts reveal) Whitman intended to use the live-oak for his key-symbol, and the pathos of his poem on this subject has pained many a sensitive reader:

I saw in Louisiana a live-oak growing,
All alone stood it, and the moss hung down from the
*   branches,*
Without any companion it grew there, uttering joyous
*   leaves of dark green,*
And its look, rude, unbending, lusty, made me think of
*   myself,*
But I wondered how it could utter joyous leaves, standing
*   alone there, without its friend, its lover near—*
*   for I knew I could not.*
And I broke off a twig with a certain number of leaves
*   upon it, and twined around it a little moss,*
And brought it away—and I have placed it in sight in my
*   room,*
It is not needed to remind me as of my own dear friends,
(For I believe lately I think of little else than of them),
Yet it remains to me a curious token—it makes me think
*   of manly love;*
For all that, and though the live-oak glistens there in
*   Louisiana, solitary, in a wide flat space,*
Uttering joyous leaves all its life, without a friend, a
*   lover, near,*
I know very well I could not.

The same sense of loneliness and longing for a responsive friend and/or lover runs throughout many of the "Calamus" poems, and was no doubt an expression of intimate emotions. But, as with the "Enfans d'Adam" poems, this love-friendship motif also can be applied symbolically, for in 1860, when the United States was tottering on the brink of the greatest civil war in history (as Whitman had predicted in "The Eighteenth Presidency," though in 1860 he did not realize how near his prophecy was to fulfillment), something more than "an agreement on a paper" was indeed needed to hold the States together.

States!
Were you looking to be held together by the lawyers?
By an agreement on a paper? Or by arms?

Away!
I arrive, bringing these, beyond all the forces of courts
*   and arms,*
These! to hold you together as firmly as the earth itself
*   is held together.*

By "these" he meant his poems, perhaps specifically his "Calamus" poems, for:

There shall from me be a new friendship—It shall be
*   called after my name,*
It shall circulate through The States, indifferent of place,
It shall twist and intertwist them through and around each
*   other—Compact shall they be, showing new signs,*
Affection shall solve every one of the problems of freedom,
Those who love each other shall be invincible,
They shall finally make America completely victorious,
*   in my name.*

In retrospect this seems one of the most ironical passages in any edition of *Leaves of Grass*. The "new friendship" and affection did not "circulate through The States," or solve any of their problems, and even the distribution of Whitman's book was halted by the bankruptcy of his publishers soon after the outbreak of war between The States.

Changes of Garments

Agonies are one of my changes of garments,
I do not ask the wounded person how he feels,
I myself become the wounded person,
My hurt turns livid upon me . . .

"...SO SHRILL YOU BUGLES BLOW"

During the summer of 1860 and the following winter, Whitman had no foreboding of disaster, personal or national. His book was selling well enough to encourage him and his publisher to plan a new volume, which Thayer & Eldridge announced as *Banner at Day-Break.* One of the new poems to be included in this volume was "Errand-Bearers" (later: "A Broadway Pageant"), written in celebration of a parade of visiting Japanese envoys up Broadway on June 16. While Whitman was still in Boston they had arrived in Washington to conclude a treaty with the United States, as a consequence of Admiral Perry's forcing open Japan's "closed door." Whitman shared the excitement of everyone in the City:

> *When million-footed Manhattan, unpent, descends to her*
> *pavements, . . .*
> *When the thunder-cracking guns arouse me with the*
> *proud roar I love,*
> . . . .
> *I too arising, answering, descend to the pavements, merge*
> *with the crowd, and gaze with them.*

But the poet also saw in this event the prophecy of a new era of world commerce, peace, and liberty, perhaps the fulfillment of God's plan from the beginning:

> —*Were the children straying westward so long? So wide the tramping?*
> *Were the precedent dim ages debouching westward from Paradise so long? . . .*
> . . . .
> *They shall now march obediently eastward, for your sake, Libertad.*

Meanwhile, Whitman's life went on much as usual, hob-nobbing with the Pfaff crowd, riding the Broadway stages with his friends the drivers and conductors—sometimes collecting fares for them, or even driving in the absence of a sick driver—and watching with keenest interest the Presidential nominations and campaigns of 1860. He admired Senator Douglas and was slow to recognize in Lincoln the ideal candidate he had described in "The Eighteenth Presidency."

After the election, Lincoln passed through hostile New York on his way to Washington to be inaugurated. On February 18, 1861, Whitman happened to be riding past the Astor House on top of an omnibus when Lincoln alighted from his barouche and calmly surveyed the sullen crowd: "I had . . . a capital view of it all, and especially of Mr. Lincoln, his look and gait—his perfect composure and coolness—his unusual and uncouth height, his dress of complete black, stovepipe hat push'd back on his head, darkbrown complexion, seam'd and wrinkled yet canny-looking face, black, bushy head of hair, disproportionately long neck, and his hands held behind as he stood observing the people. He look'd with curiosity upon that immense sea of faces, and the sea of faces return'd the look with similar curiosity. In both there was a dash of comedy, almost farce, such as Shakespeare puts in his blackest tragedies. The crowd that hemm'd around consisted I should think of thirty to forty thousand men, not a single one his personal friend—while I have no doubt (so frenzied were the ferments of the time), many an assassin's knife or pistol lurk'd in hip or breast-pocket there, ready, soon as break or riot came."

On the night of April 12, Whitman went to the opera on Fourteenth Street. Walking down Broadway on his way to the Brooklyn ferry, he heard "loud cries of the newsboys, who came presently tearing and yelling up the street, rushing from side to side even more furiously than usual." They were selling the morning papers, dated April 13, with banner headlines about the firing on Fort Sumter and the United States flag in Charleston harbor, South Carolina. "I bought an extra and cross'd to the Metropolitan hotel (Niblo's), where the great lamps were still brightly blazing, and, with a crowd of others, who gather'd impromptu, read the news, which was evidently authentic. For the benefit of some who had no papers, one of us read the telegram aloud, while all listened silently and attentively. No remark was made by any of the crowd, which had increas'd to thirty or forty, but all stood a minute or two, I remember, before they dispers'd."

George Whitman enlisted almost immediately with the Thirteenth Regiment, which trained near the national capital. Almost everyone in New York and Brooklyn thought the rebellion would be crushed in a few days or weeks. But, as Whitman wrote, "All this sort of feeling was destin'd to be arrested and revers'd by a terrible shock—the battle of first Bull Run." Washington was thrown into "a mixture of awful consternation, uncertainty, rage, shame, helplessness, and stupefying disappointment."

Although Whitman was in Brooklyn and could follow the events only through the newspapers, which he eagerly read one after another, he later wrote an account so vivid that one would think it written by an eye-witness. "The Saturday and Sunday of the battle (20th, 21st [of July]) had been parch'd and hot to an extreme—the dust, the grime and smoke, in layers, sweated in . . . all the men with this coating of murk and sweat and rain, now recoiling back, pouring over the Long Bridge—a horrible march of twenty miles, returning to Washington baffled, humiliated, panic-struck."

"The sun rises, but shines not. The men appear, at first sparsely
and shame-faced enough, then thicker, in the streets of Washington," then in mobs, squads, stragglers, even in regiment. They
drop anywhere and sleep with exhaustion. Some people, but not
many, hand out food. Some prepare coffee. The officers gather
at Willard's hotel. Many people blame them for the debacle.

Then President Lincoln sets about reorganizing his forces,
and "the great New York papers" rally the nation with "magnifi-
cent editorials! they never flagg'd for a fortnight." Why did Walt
Whitman himself not enlist at the height of his own emotional
reaction? The question has often been raised. There are two
good answers: he was forty-two years old, though he looked
much older, and this was, like most wars, a young man's war.
Besides he had to support his mother and dependent brother Eddie. But he did make a contribution a few weeks later, and not an
insignificant one, by writing a recruiting poem, "Beat! Beat!
Drums!," which was published simultaneously on September 28,
in the *New York Leader* and the popular *Harper's Weekly*.

> *Beat! beat! drums—Blow! bugles! blow!*
> *Through the windows—through doors—burst like a force*
>   *of ruthless men,*
> *Into the solemn church, and scatter the congregation;*
> *Into the school where the scholar is studying:*
> *Leave not the bridegroom quiet—no happiness must he*
>   *have now with his bride;*
>
> *Nor the peaceful farmer any peace, plowing his field or*
>   *gathering his grain;*
> *So fierce you whirr and pound, you drums—so shrill you*
>   *bugles blow.*
> . . . .
> *Beat! beat! drums—Blow! bugles! blow!*
> *Make no parley—stop for no expostulation;*
> *Mind not the timid—mind not the weeper or prayer;*
> *Mind not the old man beseeching the young man;*
> *Let not the child's voice be heard, nor the mother's*
>   *entreaties;*

> *Make even the trestles to shake the dead, where they lie*
> * awaiting the hearses,*
> *So strong you thump, O terrible drums—so loud you*
> * bugles blow.*

But another short poem, however, best indicates what the first year of the war meant to Whitman emotionally:

> *Year that trembled and reel'd beneath me!*
> *Your summer wind was warm enough, yet the air I*
> * breathed froze me,*
> *A thick gloom fell through the sunshine and darken'd me,*
> *Must I change my triumphant songs? said I to myself,*
> *Must I indeed learn to chant the cold dirges of the baffled?*
> *And sullen hymns of defeat?*

To prevent his family from worrying, George wrote back cheerful letters from the front, which did not deceive anyone. His danger, in fact, added suspense to the war news, and thickened the gloom of his brother the poet. Walt's journalistic writings of this period, mostly free-lancing, were not concerned with the war, but he had been visiting New York Hospital for several years, especially when omnibus drivers were ill. Some of the wounded from Bull Run were sent to this hospital to recuperate, and talking with them gave Whitman a more intimate feeling for the men doing the fighting.

"THE WOUND-DRESSER"

George Whitman distinguished himself in the storming of the Confederate fort at Roanoke, North Carolina, in February, 1862, and was promoted to the rank of second lieutenant, and to first lieutenant after the second battle of Bull Run. In December he was in the fighting at Fredericksburg, Virginia, and received a superficial wound in the cheek. Walt saw his name (garbled) in a list of wounded printed in the New York *Herald* on December 16, and rushed down to Fredericksburg to find him. He remained in camp for nine days and became thoroughly familiar with the life of the soldiers, which he recorded in copious notes. For example:

FALMOUTH, Va., opposite Fredericksburgh, December 21, 1862.—Begin my visits among the camp hospitals in the army of the Potomac. Spend a good part of the day in a large brick mansion on the banks of the Rappahannock, used as a hospital since the battle—seems to have received only the worst cases. Out doors, at the foot of a tree, within ten yards of the front of the house, I notice a heap of amputated feet, legs, arms, hands, &c., a full load for a one-horse cart. Several dead bodies lie near, each covered with its brown woolen blanket. In the door-yard, toward the river, are fresh graves, mostly officers, their names on pieces of barrelstaves or broken boards, stuck in the dirt. . . . The large mansion is quite crowded upstairs and down, everything impromptu, no system, all bad enough, but I have no doubt the best that can be done; all wounds pretty bad, some frightful, the men in their old clothes, unclean and bloody. Some of the wounded are rebel soldiers and officers, prisoners. . . .

A few days later:

December 23 to 31.—The results of the late battle are exhibited everywhere about here in thousands of cases, (hundreds die every day), in the camp, brigade, and division hospitals. These are merely tents, and sometimes very poor ones, the wounded lying on the ground, lucky if their blankets are spread on layers of pine or hemlock twigs, or small leaves. No cots; seldom even a mattress. It is pretty cold. The ground is frozen hard, and there is occasional snow. I go around from one case to another. I do not see that I do much good to these wounded and dying; but I cannot leave them. Once in a while some youngster holds on to me convulsively, and I do what I can for him; at any rate, stop with him and sit near him for hours, if he wishes it.

Besides the hospitals, I also go occasionally on long tours through the camps, talking with the men, &c. Sometimes at

night among the groups around the fires, in their shebang
enclosures of bushes . . . Sometimes I go down on picket
with regiments I know best. . . .

Whitman found little he could do except talk with the sick
and wounded and write letters home for those unable to write.
On December 28, he returned to Washington by train and boat
with a trainload of wounded men. During the trip he went among
the stretchers, carrying drinking water and taking messages from
the men to send to their families. He had found his great work.

In Washington Whitman rented inexpensive rooms, staying
first with William Douglas O'Connor, now a government employee, and his wife, Ellen, who was to become the poet's life-long
friend. Whitman's recent publisher, Charles W. Eldridge, was
now assistant to the Army Paymaster, and Eldridge got him a
job as copyist (secretary) in the Paymaster's office. The work
required only two or three hours a day, and paid only a few dollars a week, thus leaving Whitman most of the day for visiting
the wounded in the hospitals.

Although two organizations, the United States Sanitary Commission and the Christian Commission, were attempting to do
the kind of personnel work that the Salvation Army did in World
War I, they were not able to do all that was needed. Whitman
joined the latter, which paid no salary, but soon decided that he
could accomplish more on his own initiative. With meager funds
sent him by friends in Brooklyn, New York, and Boston (Emerson contributed from Concord) and the sale of a few articles to
New York and Brooklyn newspapers, Whitman bought tobacco,
fruit, stationery, and other small items that the men wanted and
methodically distributed these on frequent trips through the
wards. The spirit of his work, and the change in his attitude toward the war, Whitman expressed in a poem published later as
"The Wound-Dresser":

> *Arous'd and angry, I'd thought to beat the alarum, and*
>   *urge relentless war,*
> *But soon my fingers fail'd me, my face droop'd and I*
>   *resigned myself,*

> *To sit by the wounded and soothe them, or silently watch*
>   *the dead;*
> . . . .
>
> *The hurt and wounded I pacify with soothing hand,*
> *I sit by the restless all the dark night, some are so young,*
> *Some suffer so much, I recall the experience sweet and sad,*
> *(Many a soldier's loving arms about this neck have cross'd*
>   *and rested,*
> *Many a soldier's kiss dwells on these bearded lips.)*

The emotional and physical strain of his hospital work affected Whitman's own health, and he had occasionally to desist, even to return to Brooklyn for rest. But he always went back to Washington and took up the daily rounds again. In the summer of 1864 he wrote this description:

> I am back again in Washington, on my regular daily and nightly rounds. Of course there are many specialties. Dotting a ward here and there are always cases of poor fellows, long-suffering under obstinate wounds, or weak and dishearten'd from typhoid fever, or the like; mark'd cases, needing special and sympathetic nourishment. These I sit down and talk to, or silently cheer them up. They always like it hugely, (and so do I). Each case has its peculiarities, and needs some new adaptation. I have learnt to thus conform—learnt a good deal of hospital wisdom. Some of the poor young chaps, away from home for the first time in their lives, hunger and thirst for affection; this is sometimes the only thing that will reach their condition. The men like to have a pencil, and something to write in. I have given them cheap pocket-diaries, and almanacs for 1864, interleav'd with blank paper. For reading I generally have some old pictorial magazines or story papers—they are always acceptable. Also the morning or evening papers of the day. The best books I do not give, but lend to read through the wards, and then take them to others, and so on; they are very punctual about returning the books. In these wards, or on the field, as I thus continue to go round, I have come to adapt myself to each emergency, after its kind

or call, however trivial, however solemn, every one justified and made real under its circumstances—not only visits and cheering talk and little gifts—not only washing and dressing wounds, (I have some cases where the patient is unwilling any one should do this but me)—but passages from the Bible, expounding them, prayer at the bedside, explanations of doctrine, &c. (I think I see my friends smiling at this confession, but I was never more in earnest in my life.) In camp and everywhere, I was in the habit of reading or giving recitations to the men. They were very fond of it, and liked declamatory poetical pieces. We would gather in a large group by ourselves, after supper, and spend the time in such readings, or in talking, and occasionally by an amusing game called the game of twenty questions.

For some of these men Whitman developed a deep, paternalistic affection. One was a young sergeant named Tom Sawyer. Another was Lewis ("Lewy") Brown, who had to have a leg amputated and whom Walt nursed through the danger of hemorrhage. Many of these men never forgot the kindness of the large, graybearded man who gave them so unselfishly of his time, energy, and sympathy. And Walt himself found in his hospital ministrations the greatest satisfaction of his entire life.

31. *Walt Whitman, 1862*

32. Japanese Ambassadors, 1860

33. Great Meeting, Union Square, New York, April 20, 1861

34. *Washington, D.C., 1861. View from balloon; note unfinished Capitol dome*

35. *Thirteenth Regiment leaving Brooklyn, April 23, 1861. Whitman's brother George left with it*

36. *Battlefield near Fredericksburg, Virginia, where George Whitman was wounded, 1862*

37. *Walt Whitman, 1862*

38. Soldiers' Depot, Dining Room

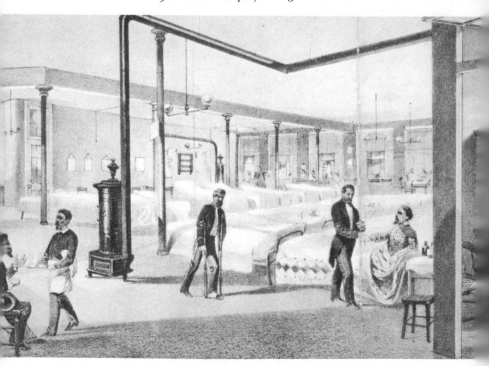

39. Soldiers' Depot, Hospital

No. 158

Office Christian Commission,

No. 13 Bank Street.

Philadelphia, Jany 20th 1863

To Officers of the Army and Navy of the United States, and others:

The **CHRISTIAN COMMISSION,** organized by a Convention of the Young Men's Christian Associations of the loyal States, to promote the spiritual and temporal welfare and improvement of the men of the Army and Navy, acting under the approbation and commendation of the President, the Secretaries of the Army and the Navy, and of the Generals in command, have appointed

Walt Whitman of Brooklyn N.Y.

A Delegate, to act in accordance with instructions furnished herewith, under direction of the proper officers, in furtherance of the objects of the Christian Commission.

His services will be rendered in behalf of the Christian Commission, without remuneration from, or expense to, the Government.

His work will be that of distributing stores where needed, in hospitals and camps; circulating good reading matter amongst soldiers and sailors; visiting the sick and wounded, to instruct, comfort and cheer them, and aid them in correspondence with their friends at home; aiding Surgeons on the battle-field and elsewhere in the care and conveyance of the wounded to hospitals; helping Chaplains in their ministrations and influence for the good of the men under their care; and addressing soldiers and sailors, individually and collectively, in explanation of the work of the Christian Commission and its Delegates, and for their personal instruction and benefit, temporal and eternal.

All possible facilities, and all due courtesies, are asked for him, in the proper pursuance of any or all of these duties.

Geo. H. Stuart

Chairman Christian Commission.

40. Walt Whitman's Office Christian Commission, January 20, 1863

41. Walt Whitman, Washington, D.C., 1863

🌿 *Memories of Lincoln*

When lilacs last in the dooryard bloom'd,
And the great star early droop'd in the western sky in
the night,
I mourn'd, and yet shall mourn with ever-returning spring.

DEATH OF LINCOLN

During the hot summer of 1864 Whitman suffered so frequently from headaches and dizziness that he was forced to return
to Brooklyn for rest and recuperation. Early in December he had
to commit his oldest brother, Jesse, to an insane asylum. And the
day after Christmas George's trunk arrived, with the personal
possessions he had carried around with him in the Army. "It
made us feel pretty solemn," Walt recorded in a memorandum.
"We have not heard from him since October 3rd; whether living
or dead we know not. I am aware of the condition of the union
prisoners south, through seeing them when brought up. . . .
The situation, as of all men in prison, is indescribably horrible.
Hard, ghastly starvation is the rule. Rags, filth, despair in large
open stockades, no shelter, no cooking. . . ."

In January Whitman's friends in Washington, especially
O'Connor, succeeded in obtaining a position for him as clerk in
the Department of the Interior, and he hastened to report for
duty. In Washington he continued his efforts to get information
about George, and through John Swinton, managing editor of
the *New York Times*, brought pressure on General Grant to

arrange an exchange for George, now a captain (if still alive). These efforts finally paid off, and George Whitman was released from the Danville, Virginia, prison just before the second Inauguration of Lincoln on March 4, though Walt seems not to have heard the good news until after the Inauguration.

By this time Whitman was a great admirer of Lincoln, almost an idolater. At noon on Inauguration Day he saw the President ride down to the Capitol, and from the sidewalk he watched his return to the White House around three o'clock, after the ceremonies and parade were over, looking worn and tired, the "demands of life and death cut deeper than ever upon his dark brown face; yet all the old goodness, tenderness, sadness, and canny shrewdness, underneath the furrows." That evening Whitman attended the reception at the White House and was pushed and jostled through the passageways by the unruly mob, one of the maddest, most destructive crowds to attend such a function since the notorious inaugural reception for Andrew Jackson. He saw "Mr. Lincoln, drest all in black, with white kid gloves and a claw-hammer coat, receiving, as in duty bound, shaking hands, looking very disconsolate, and as if he would give anything to be somewhere else." Apparently he himself did not shake hands with the President.

Soon after learning of George's arrival in Brooklyn, Walt applied for and obtained a leave from his position. Around the middle of March he joined his brother in Brooklyn, and he was still there on Good Friday, April 14, when Lincoln was assassinated. The Whitman family read the news in the Saturday morning newspaper. "Mother prepared breakfast—and other meals afterward—as usual; but not a mouthful was eaten all day by either of us. We each drank half a cup of coffee; that was all. Little was said. We got every newspaper morning and evening, and the frequent extras of that period, and pass'd them silently to each other."

In the afternoon Walt took the ferry to New York and walked up Broadway. In a notebook he wrote: "All Broadway is black with mourning—the facades of the houses are festooned with black—great flags with wide heavy fringes of dead black, give a pensive effect—toward noon the sky darkened & it began to rain. Drip, drip & heavy moist black weather—the stores are all closed—the rain sent the women from the street & black clothed men only remained—black clouds driving overhead—the horror, fever, uncertainty, alarm in the public—Every hour brings a great history event on the wires—at 11 o'clock the new president is sworn—at 4 the murder is [unfinished]."

Whitman's leave was due to expire the following Monday, the day after Easter, but circumstantial evidence indicates that he did not return to Washington by that date, perhaps because he had learned that his office would be closed. He may, indeed, have missed altogether seeing the President lying on a catafalque under the Capitol dome, the solemn procession through the streets with the military bands playing the dead march, and even the start of the funeral train on its slow circuit through Baltimore, Philadelphia, New York, Buffalo, Cleveland, Chicago, and on to Springfield, Illinois. But when Whitman returned to Washington, whatever the day, the lilacs were in bloom, and the shape, color, and sweet perfume of this old-fashioned flower became intertwined in his memory with the death of the great man.

While on leave in Brooklyn Whitman had made arrangements and begun printing his wartime poems, *Drum-Taps*, at his own expense. Realizing that this poetic record of the war would not be complete without a memorial poem on Lincoln, he hastily wrote and inserted four quatrains beginning "Hush'd be the camps today," which he used as title, with appended subtitle, "A. L. Buried April 19, 1865," the date of the funeral service in Washington, not the final service in Springfield. The poem was perfunctory, and gave no promise of the great elegy which he would be able to write during the coming summer. Perhaps, indeed, the event of Lincoln's death was too recent, the shock too paralyzing, for Whitman's muse. Like Wordsworth, he wrote best in the "tranquility" of memory.

As time passed, Whitman was able to bring together the events, emotions, and images of the past spring, to transform them into symbols and weld them into an elegiac structure. There was the evening star, Venus, which had seemed to communicate some portentous message a short time before that tragic, ironic Good Friday. This became the "western fallen star." In actuality, during that evening of rapport with Venus, Whitman had heard a lone bugle sounding taps, but he wanted for his poem the music of nature. His friend John Burroughs was an ornithologist, and he may have suggested the song of the hermit thrush. Anyway, this was the bird Whitman chose, and to many readers it was to seem like a true inspiration. Thus the star became in the poem a symbol of grief for the fallen hero, and the song of the bird a symbol of death in nature, which must be accepted because it is natural. For a mediating symbol of love, Whitman chose the lilac, "with heart-shaped leaves of rich green," and "pointed blossoms rising delicate, with the perfume strong I love." Finally, the death took place in spring, the time of resurrection in nature— and at Easter-time, the symbol of spiritual resurrection. These motifs, beautifully combined with the historical fact that the funeral train quite literally traveled over the breast of the continent in springtime, Whitman conveyed with a perfect blending of imagery and rhythm.

> *Over the breast of the spring, the land, amid cities,*
> *Amid lanes and through old woods, where lately the violets*
>   *peep'd from the ground, spotting the gray debris,*
> *Amid the grass in the fields each side of the lanes, passing*
>   *the endless grass,*
> *Passing the yellow-spear'd wheat, every grain from its*
>   *shroud in the dark brown fields uprisen,*
> *Passing the apple-tree blows of white and pink in the*
>   *orchards,*
> *Carrying a corpse to where it shall rest in the grave,*
> *Night and day journeys a coffin.*
>
> *Coffin that passes through lanes and streets,*
> *Through day and night with the great cloud darkening*
>   *the land,*

*With the pomp of the inloop'd flags with the cities draped
    in black,*
*With the show of the States themselves as of crape-veil'd
    women standing,*
*With processions long and winding and the flambeaus of
    the night,*
*With the countless torches lit, with the silent sea of
    faces and the unbared heads,*
*With the waiting depot, the arriving coffin, the sombre
    faces,*
*With dirges through the night, with the thousand voices
    rising strong and solemn,*
*With all the mournful voices of the dirges pour'd around
    the coffin,*
*The dim-lit churches and the shuddering organs—where
    amid these you journey,*
With the tolling bells' perpetual clang,
Here, coffin that slowly passes,
I give you my sprig of lilac.

END OF THE WAR

Walt Whitman himself was aware at the time that 1865 was one
of the most momentous years in his life as well as in American
history. The end of the war had come early in April not long
after Lincoln's death and Whitman returned to Washington to
find the new President, Andrew Johnson, already embroiled in
the turbid political struggles of "reconstruction." In May he got a
good view of President Johnson during the Grand Review of
the Union armies, which dramatized the victory of the North.
In a letter to his mother dated May 25, Whitman described the
spectacle he had seen on Pennsylvania Avenue:

> Dear Mother, . . . Well, the Review is over, & it was very
> grand—it was too much & too impressive, to be described—
> but you will see a good deal about it in the papers. If you
> can imagine a great wide avenue like Flatbush avenue, quite
> flat, & stretching as far as you can see with a great white

building half as big as Fort Greene [in Brooklyn] on a hill
at the commencement of the avenue, and then through this
avenue marching solid ranks of soldiers, 20 or 25 abreast,
just marching steady all day long for two days without in-
termission, one regiment after another, real war-torn soldiers, that have been marching & fighting for years—sometimes for an hour nothing but cavalry, just solid ranks, on
good horses, with sabres glistening & carbines hanging by
their saddles, & their clothes showing hard service, but they
mostly all good-looking hardy young men—then great
masses of guns, batteries of cannon, four or six abreast, each
drawn by six horses, with the gunners seated on the am-
munition wagons—& these perhaps a long while in passing,
nothing but batteries—(it seemed as if all the cannon in the
world were here)—then great battalions of blacks, with axes
& shovels & pick axes, (real Southern darkies, black as tar)—
then again hour after hour the old infantry regiments, the
men all sunburnt—nearly every one with some old tatter in
shreds, (that *had been* a costly and beautiful *flag*)—the
great drum corps of sixty or eighty drummers massed at
the heads of the brigades, playing away—now & then a
fine brass band,—but oftener nothing but the drums & whis-
tling fifes,—but they sounded very lively—(perhaps a band
of sixty drums & fifteen or twenty fifes playing "Lannigan's
ball")—the different corps banners, the generals with their
staffs &c—the Western Army, led by Gen. Sherman (old
Bill, the soldiers all call him)—well, dear mother, that is a
brief sketch, give you some idea of the great panorama of
the Armies that have been passing through here the last two
days.

—I saw the President several times, stood close by him, &
took a good look at him—I like his expression much—he is
very plain & substantial—it seemed wonderful that just that
plain middlingsized ordinary man, dressed all in black,
without the least badge or ornament, should be the master
of all these myriads of soldiers, the best that ever trod the
earth, with forty or fifty Major-Generals, around him or
riding by with their broad yellow-satin belts around their
waists,—and of all the artillery & cavalry,—to say nothing

of all the Forts & ships, &c. &c.—I saw Gen. Grant too several times—He is the noblest Roman of them all—none of the pictures do justice to him—about sundown I saw him riding on a large fine horse, with his hat off in answer to the hurrahs—he rode by where I stood, & saw him well, as he rode by on a slow canter, with nothing but a single orderly after him—He looks like a good man—(& I believe there is much in looks)—I saw Gen. Meade, Gen. Thomas, Secretary Stanton, & lots of other celebrated government officers & generals—but the *rank* and *file* was the greatest sight of all.

The 51st was in the line Tuesday with the 9th Corps. I saw George but did not get a chance to speak to him. He is well. George is now *Major* George W. Whitman,—has been commissioned & mustered in. (Col. Wright & Col. Shephard have done it, I think.) The 51st is over to the Old Convalescent camp, between here and Alexandria, doing provost duty. It (the old camp) is now called Augur General Hospital. . . .

SECRETARY HARLAN

In many ways Whitman found the summer of 1865 very pleasant. There were visits with his brother George before he was mustered out of the Army, Sunday morning breakfasts with Mr. and Mrs. John Burroughs and long walks in the woods with John, and of course much good talk with the O'Connors in their home. *Drum-Taps* was attracting little attention, but it was still too soon to call this publishing venture a failure.

Then on June 30, like a bolt of lightning, Whitman received a notice from James Harlan, Secretary of the Interior, that his services would be "dispensed with from and after this date." The official explanation given was the need for economy, but when Whitman's friend J. Hubley Ashton, Assistant Attorney General, interviewed Harlan he learned that the actual reason was Whitman's authorship of *Leaves of Grass*. Whitman learned later that the copy of the third edition which he had been revising and had left in his desk after working hours had come to the attention of the Secretary, who examined it and was scandalized.

Ashton got Whitman transferred to the Attorney General's office the next day, without loss of pay, and here the matter might have rested and been forgotten had not O'Connor's temper continued to rise over the injustice of the dismissal. During the summer he wrote an impassioned and eloquent pamphlet which he published in 1866 as *The Good Gray Poet*.

This pamphlet deified Walt Whitman and defended *Leaves of Grass* as a literary masterpiece comparable to the works of Homer, Dante, and Shakespeare. But its most telling eloquence was directed against the evils of literary censorship in general. Although bombastic in language and exaggerated in biography and criticism, *The Good Gray Poet* became a landmark in the history of Whitman's lifetime battle against prudery and pious bigotry, and is still worth reading by anyone who values intellectual liberty.

Equals and Lovers

My spirit has pass'd in compassion and determination
around the whole earth,
I have look'd for equals and lovers and found them ready
for me in all lands,
I think some divine rapport has equalized me with them.

THE LEAVENED SOIL

Early in the autumn of 1865 Whitman added a sequel to his
Drum-Taps volume, consisting of twenty-three pages separately
numbered but bound in with sheets left over from the original
edition. The first poem in the "Sequel to Drum-Taps" was "When
Lilacs Last in the Dooryard Bloom'd," followed by "O Captain!
My Captain!" which was to become Whitman's most popular
and best known poem—partly because it came nearest to being
in conventional rhyme and meter. The "Sequel" also contained
"Dirge for Two Veterans," a poem which in the twentieth century has appealed to a number of composers and has been given
several musical settings.

The central theme of the "Sequel to Drum-Taps" was memorial
tribute to the war dead. But the poet was not unmindful of his
own debt to the war, which had matured his own mind, character,
and art. As he closed his volume of Civil War poems, he felt that
his songs, too, had trod the soil leavened with blood and sacrifice,
and that henceforth he would be a less provincial poet:

To the leaven'd soil they trod, calling, I sing, for the last;
(Not cities, nor man alone, nor war, nor the dead,
But forth from my tent emerging for good—loosing,
*   untying the tent-ropes);*
In the freshness, the forenoon air, in the far-stretching
*   circuits and vistas, again to peace restored,*
To the fiery fields emanative, and the endless vistas
*   beyond—to the south and the north;*
To the leaven'd soil of the general western world, to
*   attest my songs,*

. . . .

The Northern ice and rain, that began me, nourish me to
*   the end;*
But the hot sun of the South is to ripen my songs.

For several months, however, it appeared that both issues of
Drum-Taps would be ignored by the critics. The publication of
O'Connor's *The Good Gray Poet* in January, 1866, called their
attention again to Whitman, but the immediate reaction was un-
favorable. In reviewing *The Good Gray Poet* R. H. Stoddard in
the *Round Table* (January 20, 1866) said that Harlan "deserved
and deserves to be pilloried in the contempt of thinking men for
his wanton insult to literature in the person of Mr. Whitman."
Nevertheless this critic wrote flippantly and sarcastically of the
poet and his defender. The most supercilious of all reviews was
written by young Henry James for the *Nation*, though his comments applied more to earlier poems in *Leaves of Grass* than those
in *Drum-Taps*, and in later years he regretted having written this
review.

In general, the critics pounced upon hapless Harlan, but failed
to see Whitman's merits as a poet. In fact, the only really favorable reviews in this country were written by personal friends. In
the Boston *Commonwealth* Frank Sanborn called attention to
Whitman's valuable work in the hospitals during and after the
war, and declared, "The complaints made of his earlier poems,
that they were coarse and immoral in passages, will not apply
to this little volume, which is as free from reproach on this score

as Mr. Harlan's hymn-book." The best of all reviews was a lengthy one by John Burroughs in the *Galaxy*, a new magazine in New York. He perceived that the rhythms of "When Lilacs Last . . . " were "Like intricate and involved music, with subtle, far-reaching harmonies."

Whitman's employers also showed increasing appreciation of his services. Three men held the office of Attorney General during the first year and a half of his employment in this department, and all were pleased with his work. The third, James Speed, used him on at least one occasion to revise and finish a speech on Lincoln for him, Speed saying that he could "do it better than any man I know."

RECOGNITION IN ENGLAND

During the cold winter of 1867 Whitman was still living in an unheated, almost unfurnished room in Washington, using his meager income to help his mother, still residing unhappily in Brooklyn, and to print the poems that no publisher seemed to want—he printed a new edition of *Leaves of Grass* in 1867, to which he added *Drum-Taps*. But the personal discomforts could be ignored when proof began to arrive of recognition in England. Moncure D. Conway, who had visited him in Brooklyn in 1855 on Emerson's recommendation, had already published a long, somewhat inaccurate biographical article in the October, 1866, *Fortnightly Review*. But what excited Whitman and his friends was a long article in the summer of 1867 in the *London Chronicle* by William Michael Rossetti, brother of the more famous Dante Gabriel Rossetti. Even some American editors began to be impressed by this praise from a Rossetti in England. And most important of all was that Rossetti's interest in *Leaves of Grass* led him to suggest that he edit a selected volume of Whitman's poems for British readers. Whitman readily agreed and sent him a copy of his 1867 edition, but insisted that none of the poems or passages be expurgated. Eventually, however, he consented to a few omissions, and this fact, plus Rossetti's frank comment in his Introduction on the poet's terms, "absurd or ill-constructed words," and style sometimes "obscure, fragmentary, and agglomerative," took the edge off Whitman's satisfaction over being published in England. But this edition was to be the turning point in his struggle for recognition, though some of the results would not be known to him for several years. One result was an article published in Germany by Ferdinand Freiligrath, who happened to be an exile in England at the time the Rossetti edition appeared. This was Whitman's first introduction to Germany, which later was to have three separate periods of almost blind worship of his poems.

DEMOCRATIC VISTAS

The publicity given in the American press to Rossetti's London *Chronicle* article was probably responsible for the decision of the editors of the *Galaxy*, William C. and Francis P. Church, to invite Whitman to contribute to their magazine, though both Burroughs and O'Connor had already urged them to do so. At any rate in August Whitman sent them a poem, "A Carol of Harvest for 1867," which they accepted and urged him to write a reply to Carlyle's "Shooting Niagara: And After?" in which the dour Scot predicted that the rise of democracy, as seen in the United States, would destroy civilized culture.

Carlyle's article had angered Whitman, and he began his essay to contradict him, but as he worked on the problem he came to agree with at least part of the indictment. In his first article, "Democracy," published in the December number of the *Galaxy*, he admitted: "Society, in these States, is canker'd, crude, superstitious, and rotten . . . Never was there, perhaps, more hollowness at heart than at present . . . The depravity of the business classes of our country is not less than has been supposed, but infinitely greater . . . our New World democracy . . . [despite its] materialistic development . . . is, so far, an almost complete failure in its social aspects." This, we should remember, was written in the autumn of 1867, during the confused "reconstruction" period, when Andrew Johnson was under fire from a vindictive Congress, which finally tried to impeach him.

Though Whitman had to agree with Carlyle on some of the symptoms of contemporary democracy in the United States, he still believed basically in the soundness of the American people. In the recent war, he said, he had observed that the "unnamed, unknown rank and file" had constantly shown courage, steadfastness to duty, and borne the "lash of death," in the face of the "hopelessness, mismanagement, defeat" of their leaders. Democracy, he pointed out, was not an accomplished fact but a method of educating men to govern themselves, or in his own words, it "supplies a training school for making first-class men." In a democracy even failures may provide experience for future improvements, and the avoidance of previous mistakes. This was a *pragmatic* philosophy of society and politics before that word had been introduced by William James—though Whitman's "pragmatism" was more like John Dewey's than William James's.

In a second article, called "Personalism," Whitman amplified his theory of the dependence of political health on the development of each individual to the utmost of his potentialities. Both essays were written in an involved, digressive style that made them hard going for the average reader. This was partly the result of Whitman's pioneering thought, and partly his incapacity for abstract language; in his poetry he had always used the most concrete imagery. But whether fault of style or the unwillingness of readers to face up to the truth of Whitman's analysis, the fact is that these articles did not meet with wide approval, or even arouse much public interest.

Whitman had planned to write a third article on "Literature," showing how art and literature could be used to create and exhibit models of character and thus influence the development of the kind of men and women needed for a strong, healthy, growing, democratic society. This article the *Galaxy* did not publish, but Whitman salvaged the major ideas when he reworked the essays for publication in 1871 in the book which he called *Democratic Vistas*. With all its faults of style and organization, this little book was, and still is, a major contribution to the philosophy of democracy.

HIGH PLATEAU

In the autumn of 1863, while recuperating in Brooklyn and taking stock of his life, Walt Whitman had written to his friend in Washington, Charles W. Eldridge: "I feel to devote myself more and more to the work of my life, which is making poems . . . I shall range along the high plateau of my life and capacity for a few years now, & then swiftly descend." This was an almost clairvoyant prediction, except that the "high plateau" was nearer 1868 than 1863. In the previous year he had brought out his fifth edition of *Leaves of Grass;* in 1868 he had completed the magazine version of *Democratic Vistas* and written several major poems, including "Proud Music of the Storm," and "Thou Vast Rondure, Swimming in Space," incorporated the following year into "Passage to India," his last major poem.

The best magazines also began to pay good prices for his poems in 1868: one hundred dollars from the *Atlantic Monthly* for "Proud Music of the Storm"; twenty dollars for "Thou Vast Rondure . . . " from the *Fortnightly Review,* edited by John Morley, who had called on Whitman in Washington (though he never printed the poem he bought); and fifty dollars from the *Broadway Magazine* (London) for "Whispers of Heavenly Death." In his *William Blake* (1868) Swinburne called the elegy on Lincoln ("Lilacs") "the most sweet and sonorous nocturne ever chanted in the church of the world." He also compared Whitman and Blake, which he said was a compliment to both poets.

It was about this time, too, that Whitman found the greatest satisfaction in his friendships. His relationships with Burroughs, O'Connor, Eldridge, Ashton (who remained completely loyal after getting him transferred to the Attorney General's office), and a few other men of intellect and position, were at their best.

At the same time he had a very close friendship with a young

Irishman named Peter Doyle, a streetcar conductor whom he had met one stormy winter night in 1865 or 1866. Although Doyle had served in the Confedrate Army, he was only eighteen or nineteen when Whitman met him. He had practically no education, but was good-natured, companionable, and grateful for the advice and affection of an older man. Whitman became strongly attached to him, and they saw each other daily for several years, except when Whitman was on vacation in New York, and then he wrote frequent letters. When Pete was ill or depressed Whitman worried about him, helped him with money and other gifts. He seems, in fact, to have been a substitute son for the poet.

But Whitman was not without women friends, too, though they were never quite as close to him as Peter Doyle. Mrs. Helen Price was a motherly woman whom Whitman had known since the 1850's, when she was a neighbor of the Whitmans. Walt corresponded with her while he was in Boston in 1860, and wrote her frequently from Washington. Sometimes he boarded with her on his vacations to New York, when his mother did not have room for him. She was an intelligent woman, of high moral integrity, interested in the women's rights movement, and always a loyal admirer of Whitman as man and poet.

In Washington Mrs. Ellen O'Connor was Whitman's closest woman friend. But Mrs. Ashton liked him too. And though Mrs. Burroughs did not, she found his charm hard to resist.

"RAPPORT"

The strangest of all Whitman's friendships was with Mrs. Anne Gilchrist, widow of Alexander Gilchrist, the distinguished biographer of Blake. She was a friend of the Rossettis, the Carlyles, and Tennyson. She became so interested in William Rossetti's selections of Whitman's poem that the editor loaned her his copy of the complete *Leaves of Grass*—the 1867 edition that Whitman had sent him. In the "Calamus" poems the poet seemed to be pleading for a love that she immediately felt she could give. Without realizing the nature of her enthusiasm, Rossetti sent

Whitman a critical appreciation she had written, and he responded with books and a photograph of himself, which Rossetti passed on to her, and a correspondence ensued. From the beginning Whitman was appalled by its warmth. This is the language she used in her first letter: " . . . This is what happened to me when I read for a few days, nay, hours, in your books. It was the divine soul embracing mine. I never before dreamed what love meant: not what life meant. Never was alive before—no words but those of 'new birth' can hint the meaning of what then happened to me."

Even in this first letter (September 3, 1871) Mrs. Gilchrist made it plain that she was proposing marriage. She hoped, she said, to hear, "My Mate. The one I so much want. Bride, Wife, indissoluble eternal!" And, "Dear Walt. It is a sweet & precious thing, this love; it clings so close, so close to the Soul and Body, all so tenderly dear, so beautiful, so sacred. . . ."

Evidently Whitman did not know what to reply, so he wrote nothing for several weeks, during which he received two more letters from Mrs. Gilchrist. Finally on November 3, 1871, he wrote a letter which was a masterpiece of tact:

> I have been waiting quite a while for time and the right mood, to answer your letter in a spirit as serious as its own, and in the same unmitigated trust and affection. But more daily work than ever has fallen to me to do the present season, and though I am well and contented, my best moods seem to shun me. I wish to give to it a day, a sort of Sabbath, or holy day, apart to itself, under serene and propitious influences, confident that I could then write you a letter which would do you good, and me too. But I must at least show without further delay that I am not insensible to your love. I too send you my love. And do you feel no disappointment because I now write so briefly. My book is my best letter, my response, my truest explanation of all. In it I have put my body and spirit. You understand this better and fuller and clearer than any one else. And I too fully and clearly understand the loving letter it has evoked. Enough that

there surely exists so beautiful and a delicate relation, accepted by both of us with joy.

Whitman was caught in a dilemma of his own making. For years he had been insisting that his book was more a man's life than a book, and now a woman of intelligence, education, social distinction, and moderate wealth had literally done what he had asked but really did not want. The poems were, after all, poems to be experienced vicariously, not to be taken literally. Mrs. Gilchrist understood the meaning of Whitman's reply, and she did not write again with quite so naive frankness; yet she could not reconcile herself to a rejection of her proposal. Seeing this, Whitman finally wrote her on March 20, 1872, with painful bluntness: "Let me warn you about myself and yourself also. You must not construct such an unauthorized and imaginary figure and call it W. W., and so devotedly invest your loving nature in it. The actual W. W. is a very plain personage and entirely unworthy such devotion."

Mrs. Gilchrist denied having received this letter, but her subsequent replies indicated that she had—whether willfully deceptive or tricked by her subconscious, who can say? Whitman tried to be kind to her by sending books, newspapers, clippings, and sometimes a short note, carefully worded not to encourage her passion. Thus this strange "rapport" drifted along for several years.

DESCENT FROM THE PLATEAU

Since 1868 Whitman had been descending from the high plateau reached about that time; before long it would become a toboggan slide. Primarily, the chief difficulty was his health, but in the summer of 1870 he was also emotionally disturbed about some experience or situation which is still a mystery to biographers, though they have advanced many theories. On July 15, 1870, sitting at his desk in the Attorney General's office, Whitman scribbled this notation in ink and pencil, using two colors of each:

Congress, adjourning, is in great excitement. War is said
to be declared in Europe [at] 2½ P.M.—I am writing in
the office, not feeling very well—opprest with the heat
July 15—1870

*To give up absolutely & for good, from the present hour,
this feverish, fluctuating, useless undignified pursuit of 164*
[the numbers are written over an erasure]—*too long,
(much too long) persevered in,*—so humiliating—*It must
come at last & had better come now*—*Let there from this
hour be no faltering, no getting* [erasure] *at all henceforth,
(not once, under any circumstances)—avoid seeing her or
meeting her* [the "er" in both places written over an era-
sure] *or any talks or explanations—or any meeting whatever, from this hour forth, for life.*
July 15 '70

Since this is not a critical biography (and the author has already
speculated on this manuscript in his *The Solitary Singer*), no attempt will be made here to unravel the riddles posed by this notation. It is cited merely to demonstrate the poet's disturbed mind
—perhaps the results of a combination of causes, one of them
his physical condition. We do know from letters he wrote to
Peter Doyle from New York soon after this that he had been
pleasantly surprised to discover that Pete reciprocated his affection, having "foolishly thought it was all on the other side."

For several months following the doubts and resolutions of
July 15, 1870, life seemed to improve temporarily for Whitman.
During a ten-month leave he took from his job, he saw a new edition of *Leaves of Grass* through the press in New York, at his own
expense. This fifth edition was dated Washington, D. C., 1871,
and was reprinted in 1872 with "Passage to India" added. This
edition made practically no impression in America, but during
the winter of 1870-71 Whitman learned that Adolf Strodtmann,
with the encouragement of Freiligrath, had included translations of some of his poems in a German anthology. And in the
spring he read Swinburne's ode "To Walt Whitman in America,"

which held him up to the world as a symbol of democracy and freedom.

Also in the spring of 1872 Whitman was invited by the students of Dartmouth College (to annoy the faculty) to read a poem at commencement. He wrote and recited "As a Strong Bird on Pinions Free," the bird symbolizing American democracy, but this trite poem merely demonstrated how far the poet had fallen from his "high plateau." And his "After All, Not to Create Only" ("Song of the Exposition"), which he recited by invitation at the National Industrial Exhibition in New York the following September, was not much better. Blatantly he invited the Muse to "migrate from Greece and Ionia,"

> *Cross out please those immensely overpaid accounts,*
> *That matter of Troy and Achilles' wrath, and Aeneas',*
> *Odysseus' wanderings,*
> *Placard "Removed" and "To Let" on the rocks of your*
> *snowy Parnassus, . . .*

Later he claimed that he intended these invitations for humor, but no one at the time was amused.

From this time the descent was rapid. Whitman quarrelled with his good friend O'Connor over Negro suffrage, O'Connor wanting it extended immediately and Whitman, agreeing with President Johnson, gradually with education. Mrs. O'Connor remained Whitman's friend, but O'Connor would not speak to him. A literary quarrel in England between Robert Buchanan and Swinburne also touched Whitman. Buchanan said it was "unfortunate for Walt Whitman that he has been introduced to the English public by Mr. William Rossetti and been loudly praised by Mr. Swinburne," who had concluded "that his nastiness alone has been his recommendation." Soon after this Swinburne fiercely attacked Whitman and said his poetry was "puddled and adulterated with mere doctrine in its crudest form." Whitman took this betrayal—as he regarded it—calmly, but he was hurt nevertheless.

For some time Whitman's spells of dizziness and lassitude had been increasing in severity. On the night of January 23, 1873, while sitting at his desk in the Treasury Building (where the Attorney General had offices) he felt ill, but managed to walk home through the rain and sleet and climb the stairs to his fourth floor room. During the night he woke up to find himself paralyzed, but there was no pain, and he could not call anyone. Next morning friends came in and called a physician. Three days later he shakily wrote his mother, now staying with George and her daughter-in-law in Camden, New Jersey, this bravely reassuring letter:

> Dearest Mother,
>   I have been not well for two or three days, but am better to-day. I have had a slight stroke of paralysis, on my left side, and especially the leg—occured Thursday night last, & I have been laid up since—I am writing this in my room, 535 15th St. as I am not able to get out at present—but the doctor gives me good hopes of being out and at my work in a few days—Mother you must not feel uneasy—though I know you will—but I thought I would write & tell you the *exact truth—neither better nor worse—*
>   I have a first rate physician Dr. Drinkard—I have some very attentive friends (& if I have occasion can & will telegraph to you or George—but do not expect to have any need). . . .

42. Walt Whitman, Brooklyn, c. 1872

43. Lincoln's funeral procession, Washington D.C., 1865

44. Departure of the remains of President Lincoln

45. Grand Review, Sheridan's Cavalry on Pennsylvania Avenue, May 23, 1865

46. *Walt Whitman and a scrap of manuscript, 1868*

Congress adjourns, is in great excitement
War is said to be declared in Europe.
2½ P.M. — I am writing in the office,
not feeling very well — oppressed with the heat
July 15 — 1870

To give up absolutely &
for good, from this present hour,
this feverish, fluctuating, useless
undignified pursuit of — 16.4
— too long, (much too long) persevered in, — so humiliating —
— It must come at last &
It cannot possibly be a success
had better come now — ✻
from this hour
Let there✻ be no faltering,
or no getting — at all
henceforth (not once, under
any circumstances) — avoid
seeing her or meeting her or
any talk or explanations — or
any meeting whatever from
this hour forth, for life

July 15 '70

95

47. *Autobiographical note, Library of Congress manuscript, 1870*

48. Caricature of Walt Whitman, 1872

49. Anne Gilchrist

50. Walt Whitman with children of J. H. Johnston, 1879

51. Thomas Jefferson Whitman and his wife Mattie

. Walt Whitman, Philadelphia, 1880

53. Walt Whitman's
house, Mickle Street,
Camden, New Jersey

54. Whitman house,
Mickle Street, Cam-
den, interior

The Seas All Crossed

After the seas are all cross'd, (as they seem already
*   cross'd),*
. . . .
Finally shall come the poet worthy of that name, . . .

EBB-TIDE

Whitman did not recover from his paralytic stroke as he had
tried to make his mother think he would, though he may have
thought that he would. Mrs. Ashton tried to have him moved to
her house, but he insisted on remaining in his own room. In a
few days he did get up, but had a relapse from the exertion. In
February his sister-in-law Mattie, Jeff's wife, died, and this
greatly depressed him. His mother was also very unhappy in
Camden, and was already experiencing symptoms of the heart
failure that would soon cause her death. Late in May she became
so ill that Walt was summoned, and he was able to make the trip
by train. He arrived three days before her death on May 23,
which was the greatest emotional shock he had ever experienced.
To Peter Doyle he wrote, "It is the great cloud of my life."

After the funeral Whitman returned to Washington, and this
time accepted Mrs. Ashton's invitation to recuperate at her home.
But finally convinced that it might be weeks or months before he
could resume work, he once more went to Camden, where
George had offered him sanctuary. His brother was kind to him,
but he was a business man with no understanding of or sympathy

for a poet. Until the summer of 1874 the Government permitted Whitman to hire a substitute at a lower salary and retain the difference, but he was finally dropped from the payroll, and was then more dependent than ever, though he drew on his savings to pay board for himself and his feebleminded brother, Eddie.

But hardest of all was the loneliness. To Peter Doyle he wrote on September 26, 1873: " . . . I don't know a soul here,—am entirely alone—sometimes sit alone and think, for two hours on a stretch—have not formed a single acquaintance here, any ways intimate—My sister-in-law is very kind in all housekeeping things, cooks what I want, has first rate coffee for me and something nice in the morning, and keeps me a good bed and room— all of which is very acceptable—then, for a fellow of my size, *the friendly presence and magnetism needed*, somehow, is not here—I do not run foul of any—still I generally keep up very good heart . . . I am finishing this by the open window—still in the room where my mother died, with all the old familiar things —but all drawing to a close, as the new house is done, and I shall move on Monday."

After moving to the new house which George had built, Walt wrote again to Pete: "My brother had a large room, very handsome, on second floor, with large bay window fronting west, built for me, but I moved up here [into a small room on the third floor] instead, it is much more retired, and has the sun—I am very comfortable here indeed, but my *heart* is blank and lonesome utterly." Actually the brothers had quarrelled violently over Walt's stubbornness, and what George regarded as ingratitude.

To combat boredom the poet began writing again, poems and prose, which he sold to New York magazines and newspapers. In one poem, "Song of the Redwood Tree," for which *Harper's Magazine* paid $100, he gave expression to his own pent-up emotions in the death-chant of the tree. But he also found consolation in the identification with the tree which had filled its time and place and must now give way to "a superber race, . . . To be in them absorb'd, assimilated."

Christopher Columbus had long been one of Whitman's heroes,

and he had already written some lines for a poem on Columbus.
He now polished these off at a time when he saw a parallel between the "batter'd wreck'd old man" and himself, as he admitted
in letters to Doyle and Ellen O'Connor. Certainly he was striving
for the faith of Columbus:

> *My hands, my limbs grow nerveless;*
> *My brain feels rack'd, bewilder'd;*
> *Let the old timbers part—I will not part!*
> *I will cling fast to Thee, O God, though the waves buffet*
> * me;*
> *Thee, Thee, at least I know.*

And it was also his fond dream that some day he, too, would
be acknowledged as an explorer in the realm of literature, as
Columbus had been in geography three centuries after his un-
recognized achievements:

> *And these things I see suddenly—what mean they?*
> *As if some miracle, some hand divine unseal'd my eyes,*
> *Shadowy vast shapes smile through the air and sky,*
> *And on the distant waves sail countless ships,*
> *And anthems in new tongues I hear saluting me.*

As soon as Mrs. Gilchrist read this "sacred Poem" (and it is
indeed a religious poem), she wrote, " . . . you too have sailed
over stormy seas to your goal—surrounded with mocking disbe-
lievers—you too have paid the price of health—our Columbus."
She began yearning more than ever to join the poet, but he discouraged her, and she quietly made her own plans.

But she also began scheming ways to help Whitman financially.
When he announced a "Centennial Edition" of his *Leaves* in 1875
and a second volume of prose called *Two Rivulets* (both dated
1876), she suggested to influential friends in England that they
help the poet by buying copies. The subscription list was very impressive indeed, including nearly every writer of any consequence
in England: Tennyson, the Rossettis, George Saintsbury, Lord
Houghton, and dozens of others. These "blessed gales from the

British Isles," as Whitman called the sales, were "deep medicine" for him. However, he still opposed Mrs. Gilchrist's coming to America, perhaps not realizing how much of the "deep medicine" she had provided. Finally, on May 16, 1876, she announced that she planned to sail for Philadelphia around September 1.

Meanwhile Whitman had become acquainted with a farmer and his wife, George and Susan Stafford, who lived several miles from Camden near Timber Creek. He spent the summer of 1876 at their farm and made great progress in regaining his health, especially in improved locomotion. He was at the Stafford's when Mrs. Gilchrist arrived in America, and John Burroughs called on her for Whitman, though in a short time he did make a formal call. Later, after she had installed her family in a rented house in Philadelphia, he was her house guest many times, though the romance for which she longed never developed.

At Timber Creek Whitman spent many hours in the sunshine observing nature, taking notes, and writing little essays which later formed the latter part of *Specimen Days*. In fact, so remarkable was his improvement in health that in 1879 he was able to achieve one of his life-long ambitions to make a trip to the fabulous West. A wealthy Philadelphia newspaper publisher, Colonel John W. Forney, paid his way as far as Denver, Colorado, and back to Saint Louis, where Walt visited his brother Jeff, who was Superintendent of the Water Works. The trip merely confirmed the poet's previous theories and convictions about the West, but after seeing Platte Canyon he declared, "I have found the law of my own poems."

After his return, Whitman was invited to lecture in Boston, and did so in the spring of 1881 to an audience of writers, artists, and editors, including William Dean Howells. In the summer one of his recent but most ardent friends, Dr. Maurice Bucke, a Canadian psychiatrist, accompanied him on visits to his birthplace on Long Island and to various places in the region of New York City. In the City he had an increasing circle of friends, such as the journalist, E. C. Stedman, and the wealthy jeweler, John Johnston, whose house was always open to Whitman.

INDIAN SUMMER

For five or six years in the 1880 decade Whitman enjoyed an Indian Summer, that warm, sunshiny interval before winter closes in. He even obtained another Boston publisher, and one of great prestige, James R. Osgood. As in 1860, Whitman went up to Boston to read proof and guide his book through the press, arriving in mid-August and staying until the middle of October. These two months were quite different from the spring of 1860. Wives and sisters of his friends in Concord no longer forbade his presence. He spent a delightful week-end with Frank Sanborn and took dinner with the Emersons. By this time Emerson's memory was so decayed that he could scarcely carry on a conversation, but the poet who had once addressed him as "Master" was content to sit and look at him.

Whitman returned to Camden with the feeling that *Leaves of Grass* was finally properly published for the first time and would now take its rightful place in world literature. He had at last achieved an arrangement of the poems which he regarded as "organic" and satisfying, and would henceforth maintain. But his hopes for the Osgood edition were based on quicksand. Though his poems were attracting the attention of critics in France, Germany, Denmark, in addition to England, his bad luck with Boston publishers would continue.

In December Osgood reported, "We have printed three editions [of *Leaves of Grass*] in all, and it is selling steadily." Then on March 1, 1882, the District Attorney threatened prosecution unless two poems, "A Woman Waits for Me" and "To a Common Prostitute" were withdrawn, and some other lines deleted. Whitman refused to make any changes, and Osgood, after making a satisfactory financial settlement and turning over the plates to the author, dissociated himself from *Leaves of Grass*. Hearing that the Boston Post Office had banned the book from the mails, O'Connor went to battle once more for his friend, and either he or someone else got the ban lifted.

Whitman made an arrangement with a small publisher in

Philadelphia, Rees Welsh & Co., to take over the plates and print more copies. He had planned a volume of prose, *Specimen Days and Collect*, to be published by Osgood, and Welsh now brought out this too, in similar format and binding. This volume consisted mainly of early reminiscences, diary notes on the poet's Civil War experiences, and records of his night and days outdoors while recuperating at the Staffords. In a few months David Mc-Kay, associated with Rees Welsh, became the publisher of both books. The prose volume sold slowly, but the publicity over the suppression of the Osgood edition created a lively demand for the Rees Welsh and David McKay issues.

For several years prominent Englishmen traveling in the United States had been calling on Whitman, but in January 1882, he received a visit that gave him unusual pleasure. The caller was Oscar Wilde, then at the height of his much-publicized fame. To a reporter Whitman said after the visit, "He seemed to me like a great big, splendid boy . . . He is so frank and outspoken and manly. I don't see why so many mocking things are written about him." Of course Whitman was delighted, too, to be told that, "we in England think there are only two [American poets] —Walt Whitman and Emerson." Longfellow, said Wilde, had "contributed little to literature that might not have come just as well from European sources."

In 1884 George Whitman was planning to move out into the country into a house he had built for his family, which included Walt. But Walt had no intention of moving to the country; he could visit the Staffords when he needed country air. He preferred to remain near the Delaware River ferry, which could take him to Philadelphia in a few minutes, where he now had many friends, from bargemen to owners of newspapers. Besides, visitors, especially from England, were now arriving in increasing numbers. Consequently, with the royalties he had received from Welsh and McKay for the 1881-82 edition of *Leaves of Grass*, and a loan from George W. Childs, owner of the Philadelphia *Record*, he bought a modest little house on Mickle Street. It was near the railroad and when the wind blew from the right direction, the acrid odor of a fertilizer factory was noticeable, but the location satisfied Walt. Here he could go and come as he pleased and receive his callers in his own fashion.

LAST DAYS IN MICKLE STREET

In the Mickle Street house Whitman spent the remainder of his life. After he became so crippled that he could scarcely hobble around, the widow of a sea captain, Mrs. Mary Davis, moved in to take care of him in return for her rent. Some nosey neighbors were scandalized by this arrangement, and Mrs. Davis found it a hard bargain as the poet grew more dependent and thoughtless, but she gave him devoted care.

During his final years Whitman was greatly aided by a young man named Horace Traubel, who became his confidant, errand-boy, and recorder of his conversations—published later as *With Walt Whitman in Camden*. He brought his fiancée, Anne Montgomerie, for Walt's blessing and the couple were married in the Mickle Street house. It was Traubel, primarily, who arranged for celebrations of the poet's birthday, and when he needed constant nursing care solicited funds to pay doctors and nurses. But others helped, too, especially a young lawyer named Thomas B. Harned.

During these final years visitors from abroad continued to arrive, such as Sir Edwin Arnold, author of *The Light of Asia*, Edmund Gosse, Edward Carpenter, and others. In Bolton, England, a group of ordinary citizens who called themselves facetiously "Bolton College" sent two of their members, Dr. John Johnston and J. W. Wallace, to visit the poet and bring back a report. The report was so full and interesting that it was later published as *Visits to Walt Whitman in 1890–91 by Two Lancashire Friends*.

One of the great mysteries in Whitman's biography arose in 1890 when the poet, in reply to persistent questions from John Addington Symonds about the meaning of the "Calamus" poems, wrote: "My life, young manhood, mid-age, times South, etc., have been jolly bodily, and doubtless open to criticism. Though unmarried, I have six children, two are dead—one living Southern grandchild—fine boy writes to me occasionally—circumstances (connected with their benefit and fortune) have separated me from intimate relations." Biographers have searched for these children for half a century. Whether they were entirely imaginary may never be known.

Knowing that his life was nearing an end, Whitman wanted to get out one more edition of his *Leaves of Grass* and *Prose Works*. With Traubel's help, the edition was made ready for the press, and in the autumn of 1891, lying in bed fatally ill, he was able to hold a printed copy in his hands. His friends named this the "Death-bed Edition." A few copies were bound for distribution as Christmas presents, and the remainder in 1892.

After months of suffering, Walt Whitman died on March 26, 1892. Traubel sent the news to the "Bolton College" group, and Wallace closed his account with these words: "On the evening of Saturday, March 26th—the daylight fading and a gentle rain outside—the end came, simply and peacefully—Whitman conscious to the last, calm and undisturbed, his right hand resting in that of Horace Traubel."

An autopsy revealed that Whitman had suffered a complication of diseases severe enough to have killed a man with less stamina long before. After the autopsy the body was placed on view in the Mickle Street house. Newspapers had given large headlines to the poet's death, and hundreds of persons came, some out of sympathy, many out of curiosity. The funeral service was held under a tent at Harleigh Cemetery, with readings from *Leaves of Grass* and the scriptures of world religions. Robert Ingersoll gave an eloquent oration in which he concluded prophetically: "Long after we are dead the brave words he has spoken will sound like trumpets to the dying."

Walt Whitman was buried in a gray granite tomb which he himself had had constructed on a design borrowed from William Blake. Like the Mickle Street house and the birthplace on Long Island, it has become a shrine visited annually by many people from all parts of the world.

55. *Walt Whitman, pen drawing by Charles Duhamel*

56. *Whitman's sister-in-law Lou (Mrs. George Whitman)*

57. *Whitman's brother George*

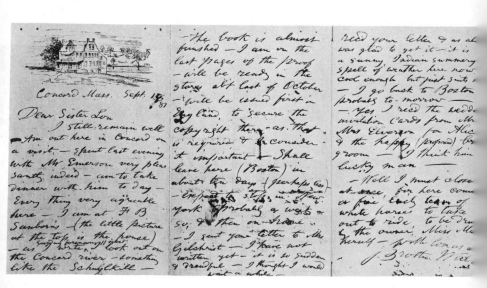

58. *Letter from Whitman to his sister-in-law Lou, 1881*

Camden Sunday aft'n July 7
Nothing very new or different
—keep up —go out in the wheel chair
—a bad spell the last week & now
(gradually declining)—a letter fm Mrs
O'C Washn. She is gloomy poorly
left without means. The little dinner
book is being put in type W W

9. Walt Whitman post card with
photograph, c. 1868, and note to Wil-
iam Sloan Kennedy, 1889

60. Horace Traubel, 1913

Dr. R. M. Bucke in his library,
um, London, Ontario, 1899

62. Walt Whitman in his house on Mickle
Street, Camden

63. Colonel Ingersoll delivering Whitman's funeral oration, 1892

ARTIST POET!

Reminiscences of Walt Whitman.

A NOBLE CHARACTER

Percy Ives' First Visit to the Author of "Leaves of Grass."

HIS SKETCH OF THE POET

Impressions Left by His Bearing, Voice, Looks, Surroundings and Conversation.

64. Reminiscences of Whitman by Percy Ives, 1896

65. Walt Whitman, sketch by Percy Ives,

66. *Walt Whitman, portrait by Herbert Gilchrist, 1886*

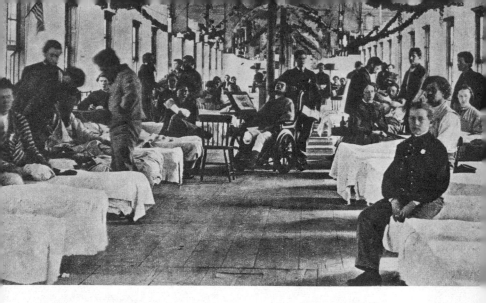

67. Union wounded in Carver Hospital, September 1864

68. Walt Whitman, portrait by Thomas Eakins, 1887

Whitman program, centenary of Leaves of Grass, Moscow, 1955

Gendai Shiika (Modern Poetry), *special Whitman number, February 1918, cover*

71. *Walt Whitman exhibit, Moscow, summer 1955*

72. *Walt Whitman Memorial, preliminary design by Jo Davidson*

EXCERPTS FROM WHITMAN

From "The 1855 Preface"

America does not repel the past or what it has produced under its forms or amid other politics or the idea of castes or the old religions . . . accepts the lesson with calmness . . . is not so impatient as has been supposed that the slough still sticks to opinions and manners and literature while the life which served its requirements has passed into the new life of the new forms . . . perceives that the corpse is slowly borne from the eating and sleeping rooms of the house . . . perceives that it waits a little while in the door . . . that it was fittest for its days . . . that its action has descended to the stalwart and wellshaped heir who approaches . . . and that he shall be fittest for his days.

The Americans of all nations at any time upon the earth have probably the fullest poetical nature. The United States themselves are essentially the greatest poem. In the history of the earth hitherto the largest and most stirring appear tame and orderly to their ampler largeness and stir. Here at last is something in the doings of man that corresponds with the broadcast doings of the day and night. Here is not merely a nation but a teeming nation of nations. Here is action untied from strings necessarily blind to particulars and details magnificently moving in vast masses. Here is the hospitality which forever indicates heroes . . . Here are the roughs and beards and space and ruggedness and nonchalance that the soul loves. Here the performance disdaining the trivial unapproached in the tremendous audacity of its crowds and groupings and the push of its perspective spreads with crampless and flowing breadth and showers its prolific and splendid extravagance. One sees it must indeed own the riches of the summer and winter, and need never be bankrupt while corn grows from the ground or the orchards drop apples or the bays contain fish or men beget children upon women.

Other states indicate themselves in their deputies . . . but the genius of the United States is not best or most in its executives or legislatures, nor in its ambassadors or authors or colleges or churches or parlors, nor even in its newspapers or inventors . . . but always most in the common people. Their manners speech dress friendships—the freshness and candor of their physiognomy —the picturesque looseness of their carriage . . . their deathless attachment to freedom—their aversion to anything indecorous or soft or mean—the practical acknowledgment of the citizens of one state by the citizens of all other states—the fierceness of their roused resentment—their curiosity and welcome of novelty —their selfesteem and wonderful sympathy—their susceptibility to a slight—the air they have of persons who never knew how it felt to stand in the presence of superiors—the fluency of their speech—their delight in music, the sure symptom of manly tenderness and native elegance of soul . . . their good temper and openhandedness—the terrible significance of their elections—the President's taking off his hat to them not they to him—these too are unrhymed poetry. It awaits the gigantic and generous treatment worthy of it.

The largeness of nature or the nation was monstrous without a corresponding largeness and generosity of the spirit of the citizen. Not nature nor swarming states nor streets and steamships nor prosperous business nor farms nor capital nor learning may suffice for the ideal of man . . . nor suffice the poet. No reminiscences may suffice either. A live nation can always cut a deep mark and can have the best authority the cheapest . . . namely from its own soul. This is the sum of the profitable uses of individuals or states and of present action and grandeur and of the subjects of poets.—As if it were necessary to trot back generation after generation to the eastern records! As if the beauty and sacredness of the demonstrable must fall behind that of the mythical! As if men do not make their mark out of any times! As if the opening of the western continent by discovery and what has transpired since in North and South America were less than the small theatre of the antique or the aimless sleepwalking of the middle ages! The pride of the United States leaves the wealth and finesse of the cities and all returns of commerce and agriculture and all the magnitude of geography or shows of exterior victory to enjoy the breed of fullsized men or one fullsized man unconquerable and simple.

The American poets are to enclose old and new for America is the race of races. Of them a bard is to be commensurate with a people. To him the other continents arrive as contributions . . . he gives them reception for their sake and his own sake. His spirit responds to his country's spirit . . . he incarnates its geography and natural life and rivers and lakes. Mississippi with annual freshets and changing chutes, Missouri and Columbia and Ohio and Saint Lawrence with the falls and beautiful masculine Hudson, do not embouchure where they spend themselves more than they embouchure into him. The blue breadth over the inland sea of Virginia and Maryland and the sea off Massachusetts and Maine and over Manhattan bay and over Champlain and Erie and over Ontario and Huron and Michigan and Superior, and over the Texan and Mexican and Floridian and Cuban seas and over the seas off California and Oregon, is not tallied by the blue breadth of the waters below more than the breadth of above and below is tallied by him. When the long Atlantic coast stretches longer and the Pacific coast stretches longer he easily stretches with them north or south. He spans between them also from east to west and reflects what is between them. On him rise solid growths that offset the growths of pine and cedar and hemlock and liveoak and locust and chestnut and cypress and hickory and limetree and cottonwood and tuliptree and cactus and wildvine and tamarind and persimmon . . . and tangles as tangled as any canebreak or swamp . . . and forest coated with transparent ice and icicles hanging from the boughs and crackling in the wind . . . and sides and peaks of mountains . . . and pasturage sweet and

free as savannah or upland or prairie . . . with flights and songs
and screams that answer those of the wildpigeon and highhold
and orchard-oriole and coot and surf-duck and redshouldered-
hawk and fish-hawk and white-ibis and indian-hen and cat-owl
and water-pheasant and qua-bird and pied-sheldrake and black-

---

Excerpt from write-up on Whitman from *Frank Leslie's Weekly*,
April 14, 1892.

ADIEU, WALT WHITMAN!

"A Great man—a great American—the most eminent
citizen of this republic—is dead," declared Colonel
Ingersoll over the bier of Walt Whitman, at the funeral
services in the Harleigh Cemetery of Camden, on the
30th ult. This exaggerated eulogy was characteristic of
its object, concerning whom his contemporaries are di-
vided between two estimates—one rejecting him altogether, the other according most enthusiastic acceptance and exalted faith.

---

bird and mockingbird and buzzard and condor and night-heron
and eagle. To him the hereditary countenance descends both
mother's and father's. To him enter the essences of the real things
and past and present events—of the enormous diversity of tem-
perature and agriculture and mines—the tribes of red aborigines
—the weatherbeaten vessels entering new ports or making land-
ings on rocky coasts—the first settlements north or south—the
rapid stature and muscle—the haughty defiance of '76, and the
war and peace and formation of the constitution . . . the union
always surrounded by blatherers and always calm and impreg-

nable—the perpetual coming of immigrants—the wharfhem'd cities and superior marine—the unsurveyed interior—the log-houses and clearings and wild animals and hunters and trappers . . . the free commerce—the fisheries and whaling and gold-digging—the endless gestation of new states—the convening of Congress every December, the members duly coming up from all climates and the uttermost parts . . . the noble character of the young mechanics and of all free American workmen and workwomen . . . the general ardor and friendliness and enterprise—the perfect equality of the female with the male . . . the large amativeness—the fluid movement of the population—the factories and mercantile life and laborsaving machinery—the Yankee swap—the New-York firemen and the target excursion—the southern plantation life—the character of the northeast and of the northwest and southwest—slavery and the tremulous spreading of hands to protect it, and the stern opposition to it which shall never cease till it ceases or the speaking of tongues and the moving of lips cease. For such the expression of the American poet is to be transcendent and new. It is to be indirect and not direct or descriptive or epic. Its quality goes through these to much more. Let the age and wars of other nations be chanted and their eras and characters be illustrated and that finish the verse. Not so the great psalm of the republic. Here the theme is creative and has vista. Here comes one among the well beloved stonecutters and plans with decision and science and sees the solid and beautiful forms of the future where there are now no solid forms.

Of all the nations the United States with veins full of poetical stuff most need poets and will doubtless have the greatest and use them the greatest. . . .

From "Song of Myself"*

[1]

I celebrate myself,
And what I assume you shall assume,
For every atom belonging to me as good belongs to you.

I loafe and invite my soul,
I lean and loafe at my ease . . . observing a spear of summer grass.

[5]

I believe in you my soul . . . the other I am must not abase itself
    to you,
And you must not be abased to the other.

Loafe with me on the grass . . . loose the stop from your throat,
Not words, not music or rhyme I want . . . not custom or lecture,
    not even the best,
Only the lull I like, the hum of your valved voice.

I mind how we lay in June, such a transparent summer morning;
You settled your head athwart my hips and gently turned
    over upon me,
And parted the shirt from my bosom-bone, and plunged your
    tongue to my barestript heart,
And reached till you felt my beard, and reached till you held
    my feet.

* These selections are from the 1855 version, which was untitled.
The section numbers have been supplied from the 1881 version.

Swiftly arose and spread around me the peace and joy and
    knowledge that pass all the art and argument of the earth;
And I know that the hand of God is the elderhand of my own,
And I know that the spirit of God is the eldest brother of my own,
And that all the men ever born are also my brothers . . . and the
    women my sisters and lovers,
And that a kelson of the creation is love;
And limitless are leaves stiff or drooping in the fields,
And brown ants in the little wells beneath them,
And mossy scabs of the wormfence, and heaped stones, and elder
    and mullen and pokeweed.

[6]

A child said, What is the grass? fetching it to me with full hands;
How could I answer the child? . . . I do not know what it is any
    more than he.

I guess it must be the flag of my disposition, out of hopeful green
    stuff woven.

Or I guess it is the handkerchief of the Lord,
A scented gift and remembrancer designedly dropped,
Bearing the owner's name someway in the corners, that we may
    see and remark, and say Whose?

Or I guess the grass is itself a child . . . the produced babe of
    the vegetation.

Or I guess it is a uniform hieroglyphic,
And it means, Sprouting alike in broad zones and narrow zones,
Growing among black folks as among white,
Kanuck, Tuckahoe, Congressman, Cuff, I give them the same,
    I receive them the same.

And now it seems to me the beautiful uncut hair of graves.

Tenderly will I use you curling grass,
It may be you transpire from the breasts of young men,
It may be if I had known them I would have loved them;

It may be you are from old people and from women, and from
    offspring taken soon out of their mother's laps,
And here you are the mothers' laps.

This grass is very dark to be from the white heads of old mothers,
Darker than the colorless beards of old men,
Dark to come from under the faint red roofs of mouths.

O I perceive after all so many uttering tongues!
And I perceive they do not come from the roofs of mouths for
    nothing.
. . . .

[21]

I am the poet of the body,
And I am the poet of the soul.

The pleasures of heaven are with me, and the pains of hell are
    with me,
The first I graft and increase upon myself . . . the latter I
    translate into a new tongue.

I am the poet of the woman the same as the man,
And I say it is as great to be a woman as to be a man,
And I say there is nothing greater than the mother of men.

I chant a new chant of dilation or pride,
We have had ducking and deprecating about enough,
I show that size is only development.

Have you outstript the rest? Are you the President?
It is a trifle . . . they will more than arrive there every one,
    and still pass on.

I am he that walks with the tender and growing night;
I call to the earth and sea half-held by the night.

Press close barebosomed night! Press close magnetic nourishing
    night!

Night of south winds! Night of the large few stars!
Still nodding night! Mad naked summer night!

Smile O voluptuous coolbreathed earth!
Earth of the slumbering and liquid trees!
Earth of departed sunset! Earth of the mountains misty-topt!
Earth of the vitreous pour of the full moon just tinged with
    blue!
Earth of shine and dark mottling the tide of the river!
Earth of the limpid gray of clouds brighter and clearer for my
    sake!
Far-swooping elbowed earth! Rich apple-blossomed earth!
Smile, for your lover comes!

Prodigal! you have given me love! . . . therefore I to you give
    love!
O unspeakable passionate love!

Thruster holding me tight and that I hold tight!
We hurt each other as the bridegroom and the bride hurt each
    other.

[24]
· ·

If I worship any particular thing it shall be some of the spread
    of my body;
Translucent mould of me it shall be you,
Shaded ledges and rests, firm masculine coulter, it shall be you,
Whatever goes to the tilth of me it shall be you,
You my rich blood, your milky stream pale strippings of my life;
Breast that presses against other breasts it shall be you,
My brain it shall be your occult convolutions,
Root of washed sweet-flag, timorous pond-snipe, nest of guarded
    duplicate eggs, it shall be you,
Mixed tussled hay of head and beard and brawn it shall be you,
Trickling sap of maple, fibre of manly wheat, it shall be you;
Sun so generous it shall be you,

Vapors lighting and shading my face it shall be you,
You sweaty brooks and dews it shall be you,
Winds whose soft-tickling genitals rub against me it shall be you,
Broad muscular fields, branches of liveoak, loving lounger in
    my winding paths, it shall be you,
Hands I have taken, face I have kissed, mortal I have ever
    touched, it shall be you.

I dote on myself . . . there is that lot of me, and all so luscious,
Each moment and whatever happens thrills me with joy.
. . . .

[29]

Blind loving wrestling touch! Sheathed hooded sharptoothed
    touch!
Did it make you ache so leaving me?

Parting tracked by arriving . . . perpetual payment of the
    perpetual loan,
Rich showering rain, and recompense richer afterward.

Sprouts take and accumulate . . . stand by the curb prolific
    and vital,
Landscapes projected masculine full-sized and golden.

[33]

Swift wind! Space! My Soul! Now I know it is true what I
    guessed at;
What I guessed when I loafed on the grass,
What I guessed while I lay alone in my bed . . . and again as I
    walked the beach under the paling stars of the morning.

My ties and ballasts leave me . . . I travel . . . I sail . . . my
    elbows rest in the sea-gaps,
I skirt the sierras . . . my palms cover continents,
I am afoot with my vision.
. . . .

Solitary at midnight in my back yard, my thoughts gone from
    me a long while,

Walking the old hills of Judea with the beautiful gentle god by
  my side;
Speeding through space . . . speeding through heaven and
  the stars,
Speeding amid the seven satellites and the broad ring and the
  diameter of eighty thousand miles,
Speeding with tailed meteors . . . throwing fire-balls, like the
  rest,
Carrying the crescent child that carries its own full mother in
  its belly;
Storming enjoying planning loving cautioning,
Backing and filling, appearing and disappearing,
I tread day and night such roads.

I visit the orchards of God and look at the spheric product,
And look at quintillions ripened, and look at quintillions green.

I fly the flight of the fluid and swallowing soul,
My course runs below the soundings of plummets.
. . . .
I am the hounded slave . . . I wince at the bite of the dogs,
Hell and despair are upon me . . . crack and again crack the
  marksmen,
I clutch the rails of the fence . . . my gore dribs thinned with
  the ooze of my skin,
I fall on the weeds and stones,
The riders spur their unwilling horses and haul close,
They taunt my dizzy ears . . . they beat me violently over
  the head with their whip-stocks.

Agonies are one of my changes of garments;
I do not ask the wounded person how he feels . . . I myself
  become the wounded person,
My hurt turns livid upon me as I lean on a cane and observe.

[44]
. . . .
My feet strike an apex of the apices of the stairs,

On every step bunches of ages, and larger bunches between the
    steps,
All below duly traveled—and still I mount and mount.

Rise after rise bow the phantoms behind me,
Afar down I see the huge first Nothing, the vapor from the
    nostrils of death,
I know I was even there . . . I waited unseen and always,
And slept while God carried me through the lethargic midst,
And took my time . . . and took no hurt from the foetic carbon.

Long I was hugged close . . . long and long.

Immense have been the preparations for me,
Faithful and friendly the arms that have helped me.

Cycles ferried my cradle, rowing and rowing like cheerful
    boatmen;
For room to me stars kept aside in their own rings,
They sent influences to look after what was to hold me.

Before I was born out of my mother generations guided me,
My embryo has never been torpid . . . nothing could overlay it,
For it the nebula cohered to an orb . . . the long slow
    strata piled to rest it on . . . vast vegetables gave it
    sustenance,
Monstrous sauroids transported it in their mouths and deposited
    it with care.

All forces have been steadily employed to complete and delight
    me,
Now I stand on this spot with my soul.

[49]
. . . .

I hear you whispering there O stars of heaven,
O suns . . . O grass of graves . . . O perpetual transfers and
    promotions . . . if you do not say anything how can I
    say anything?

Of the turbid pool that lies in the autumn forest,
Of the moon that descends the steeps of the soughing twilight,
Toss, sparkles of day and dusk . . . toss on the black stems
    that decay in the muck,
Toss to the moaning gibberish of the dry limbs.

I ascend from the moon . . . I ascend from the night,
And perceive of the ghastly glitter the sunbeams reflected,
And debouch to the steady and central from the offspring great
    or small.

[52]
The spotted hawk swoops by and accuses me . . . he complains
    of my gab and my loitering.

I too am not a bit tamed . . . I too am untranslatable,
I sound my barbaric yawp over the roofs of the world.

The last scud of day holds back for me
It flings my likeness after the rest and true as any on the
    shadowed wilds,
It coaxes me to the vapor and the dusk.

I depart as air . . . I shake my white locks at the runaway sun,
I effuse my flesh in eddies and drift it in lacy jags.

I bequeath myself to the dirt to grow from the grass I love,
If you want me again look for me under your bootsoles.

You will hardly know who I am or what I mean,
But I shall be good health to you nevertheless,
And filter and fibre your blood.

Failing to fetch me at first keep encouraged,
Missing me one place search another,
I stop some where waiting for you

From "The Sleepers"*

[1]

I wander all night in my vision,
Stepping with light feet . . . swiftly and noiselessly stepping and
    stopping,
Bending with open eyes over the shut eyes of sleepers;
Wandering and confused . . . lost to myself . . . ill-assorted . . .
    contradictory,
Pausing and gazing and bending and stopping.

How solemn they look there, stretched and still;
How quiet they breathe, the little children in their cradles.
. . . .
The earth recedes from me into the night,
I saw that it was beautiful . . . and I see that what is not the
    earth is beautiful.

I go from bedside to bedside . . . I sleep close with the other
    sleepers, each in turn;
I dream in my dream all the dreams of the other dreamers,
And I become the other dreamers.
. . . .

[8]

The sleepers are very beautiful as they lie unclothed,

---

* These selections are from the 1855 version, which was untitled.
Section numbers have been supplied from the 1881 version.

They flow hand in hand over the whole earth from east to west
  as they lie unclothed;
The Asiatic and African are hand in hand . . . the European
  and American are hand in hand,
Learned and unlearned are hand in hand . . . and male and female
  are hand in hand;
The bare arm of the girl crosses the bare breast of her lover . . .
  they press close without lust . . . his lips press her neck,
The father holds his grown or ungrown son in his arms
  with measureless love . . . and the son holds the father in
  his arms with measureless love,
The white hair of the mother shines on the white wrist of the
  daughter,
The breath of the boy goes with the breath of the man . . .
  friend is inarmed by friend,
The scholar kisses the teacher and the teacher kisses the scholar
  . . . the wronged is made right,
The call of the slave is one with the master's call . . . and the
  master salutes the slave,
The felon steps forth from the prison . . . the insane becomes
  sane . . . the suffering of sick persons is relieved,
The sweatings and fevers stop . . . the throat that was unsound
  is sound . . . the lungs of the consumptive are resumed . . .
  the poor distressed head is free,
The joints of the rheumatic move as smoothly as ever, and
  smoother than ever,
Stiflings and passages open . . . the paralysed become supple,
The swelled and convulsed and congested awake to themselves
  in condition,
They pass the invigoration of the night and the chemistry of the
  night and awake.
. . . .

From "To Think of Time"*

[1]

To think of time . . . to think through the retrospection,
To think of today . . . and the ages continued henceforward.
Have you guessed you yourself would not continue? Have you
    dreaded those earth-beetles?
Have you feared the future would be nothing to you?

Is today nothing? Is the beginningless past nothing?
If the future is nothing they are just as surely nothing.

To think that the sun rose in the east . . . that men and women
    were flexible and real and alive . . . that every thing was
    real and alive;
To think that you and I did not see feel think nor bear our part,
To think that we are now here and bear our part.

[3]

To think that the rivers will come to flow, and the snow fall, and
    fruits ripen . . . and act upon others as upon us now . . . yet
    not act upon us;
To think of all these wonders of city and country . . .
    and others taking great interest in them . . . and we taking
    small interest in them.

To think how eager we are in building our houses,

* These selections are fom the 1855 version, which was untitled.
Section numbers have been supplied from the 1881 version.

To think others shall be just as eager . . . and we quite indifferent.

I see one building the house that serves him a few years . . .
    or seventy or eighty years at most;
I see one building the house that serves him longer than that.

Slowmoving and black lines creep over the whole earth . . . they
    never cease . . . they are the burial lines,
He that was President was buried, and he that is now President
    shall surely be buried.

[4]
Cold dash of waves at the ferrywharf,
Posh and ice in the river . . . half-frozen mud in the streets,
A gray discouraged sky overhead . . . the short last daylight of
    December,
A hearse and stages . . . other vehicles give place,
The funeral of an old stagedriver . . . the cortege mostly drivers.

Rapid the trot to the cemetery,
Duly rattles the deathbell . . . the gate is passed . . . the grave is
    halted at . . . the living alight . . . the hearse uncloses,
The coffin is lowered and settled . . . the whip is laid on the
    coffin,
The earth is swiftly shovelled in . . . a minute . . . no one moves or
    speaks . . . it is done,
He is decently put away . . . is there anything more?

He was a goodfellow,
Freemouthed, quicktempered, not badlooking, able to take his
    own part,
Witty, sensitive to a slight, ready with life or death for a friend,
Fond of women, . . . played some . . . eat hearty and drank hearty,
Had known what it was to be flush . . . grew lowspirited
    toward the last . . . sickened . . . was helped by a
    contribution,
Died aged forty-one years . . . and that was his funeral.

Thumb extended or finger uplifted,
Apron, cape, gloves, strap . . . wetweather clothes . . . whip
    carefully chosen . . . boss, spotter, starter, and hostler,
Somebody loafing on you, or you loafing on somebody . . .
    headway . . . man before and man behind,
Good day's work or bad day's work . . . pet stock or mean stock
    . . . first out or last out . . . turning in at night,
To think that these are so much and so nigh to other drivers . . .
    and he there takes no interest in them.
. . . .

TO THE GARDEN THE WORLD

To the garden the world anew ascending,
Potent mates, daughters, sons, preluding,
The love, the life of their bodies, meaning and being,
Curious here behold my resurrection after slumber,
The revolving cycles in their wide sweep having brought me
    again,
Amorous, mature, all beautiful to me, all wondrous,
My limbs and the quivering fire that ever plays through them,
    for reasons, most wondrous,
Existing I peer and penetrate still,
Content with the present, content with the past,
By my side or back of me Eve following,
Or in front, and I following her just the same.

IN PATHS UNTRODDEN

In paths untrodden,
In the growth by margins of pond-waters,
Escaped from the life that exhibits itself,
From all the standards hitherto publish'd, from the pleasures,
    profits, conformities,
Which too long I was offering to feed my soul,

Clear to me now standards not yet publish'd, clear to me that my
    soul,
That the soul of the man I speak for rejoices in comrades,
Here by myself away from the clank of the world,
Tallying and talk'd to here by tongues aromatic,
No longer abash'd, (for in this secluded spot I can respond as I
    would not dare elsewhere,)
Strong upon me the life that does not exhibit itself, yet contains
    all the rest,
Resolv'd to sing no songs to-day but those of manly attachment,
Projecting them along that substantial life,
Bequeathing hence types of athletic love,
Afternoon this delicious Ninth-month in my forty-first year,
I proceed for all who are or have been young men,
To tell the secret of my nights and days,
To celebrate the need of comrades.

I SAW IN LOUISIANA A LIVE-OAK GROWING

I saw in Louisiana a live-oak growing,
All alone stood it and the moss hung down from the branches,
Without any companion it grew there uttering joyous leaves of
    dark green,
And its look, rude, unbending, lusty, made me think of myself,
But I wonder'd how it could utter joyous leaves standing alone
    there without its friend near, for I knew I could not,
And I broke off a twig with a certain number of leaves upon it,
    and twined around it a little moss,
And brought it away, and I have placed it in sight in my room,
It is not needed to remind me as of my own dear friends,
(For I believe lately I think of little else than of them,)
Yet it remains to me a curious token, it makes me think of
    manly love;
For all that, and though the live-oak glistens there in Louisiana
    solitary in a wide flat space,
Uttering joyous leaves all its life without a friend a lover near,
I know very well I could not.

WHEN I HEARD AT THE CLOSE OF THE DAY

When I heard at the close of the day how my name had been
    receiv'd with plaudits in the capitol, still it was not a
    happy night for me that follow'd,
And else when I carous'd, or when my plans were accomplish'd,
    still I was not happy,
But the day when I rose at dawn from the bed of perfect health,
    refresh'd, singing, inhaling the ripe breath of autumn,
When I saw the full moon in the west grow pale and disappear
    in the morning light,
When I wander'd alone over the beach, and undressing bathed,
    laughing with the cool waters, and saw the sun rise,
And when I thought how my dear friend my lover was on his
    way coming, O then I was happy,
O then each breath tasted sweeter, and all that day my food
    nourish'd me more, and the beautiful day pass'd well,
And the next came with equal joy, and with the next at evening
    came my friend,
And that night while all was still I heard the waters roll slowly
    continually up the shores,
I heard the hissing rustle of the liquid and sands as directed to
    me whispering to congratulate me,
For the one I love most lay sleeping by me under the same
    cover in the cool night,
In the stillness in the autumn moonbeams his face was inclined
    toward me,
And his arm lay lightly around my breast—and that night I
    was happy.

A NOISELESS PATIENT SPIDER

A noiseless patient spider,
I mark'd where on a little promontory it stood isolated,
Mark'd how to explore the vacant vast surrounding,

It launch'd forth filament, filament, filament, out of itself,
Ever unreeling them, ever tirelessly speeding them.

And you O my soul where you stand,
Surrounded, detached, in measureless oceans of space,
Ceaselessly musing, venturing, throwing, seeking the spheres to
    connect them,
Till the bridge you will need be form'd, till the ductile anchor
    hold,
Till the gossamer thread you fling catch somewhere, O my soul.

A SIGHT IN CAMP IN THE DAYBREAK
GRAY AND DIM

A sight in camp in the daybreak gray and dim,
As from my tent I emerge so early sleepless,
As slow I walk in the cool fresh air the path near by the hospital
    tent,
Three forms I see on stretchers lying, brought out there untended
    lying,
Over each the blanket spread, ample brownish woolen blanket,
Gray and heavy blanket, folding, covering all.

Curious I halt and silent stand,
Then with light fingers I from the face of the nearest the first
    just lift the blanket;
Who are you elderly man so gaunt and grim, with well-gray'd
    hair, and flesh all sunken about the eyes?
Who are you my dear comrade?

Then to the second I step—and who are you my child and
    darling?
Who are you sweet boy with cheeks yet blooming?

Then to the third—a face nor child nor old, very calm, as of
    beautiful yellow-white ivory;
Young man I think I know you—I think this face is the face of
    the Christ himself,
Dead and divine and brother of all, and here again he lies.

SPARKLES FROM THE WHEEL

Where the city's ceaseless crowd moves on the livelong day,
Withdrawn I join a group of children watching, I pause aside
  with them.

By the curb toward the edge of the flagging,
A knife-grinder works at his wheel sharpening a great knife,
Bending over he carefully holds it to the stone, by foot and knee,
With measur'd tread he turns rapidly, as he presses with light
  but firm hand,
Forth issue then in copious golden jets,
Sparkles from the wheel.

The scene and all its belongings, how they seize and affect me,
The sad sharp-chinn'd old man with worn clothes and broad
  shoulder-band of leather,
Myself effusing and fluid, a phantom curiously floating, now
  here absorb'd and arrested,
The group, (an unminded point set in a vast surrounding,)
The attentive, quiet children, the loud, proud, restive base of
  the streets,
The low hoarse purr of the whirling stone, the light-press'd
  blade,
Diffusing, dropping, sideways-darting, in tiny showers of gold,
Sparkles from the wheel.

TO A LOCOMOTIVE IN WINTER

Thee for my recitative,
Thee in the driving storm even as now, the snow, the winter-day
  declining,
Thee in thy panoply, thy measur'd dual throbbing and thy beat
  convulsive,
Thy black cylindric body, golden brass and silvery steel,

Thy ponderous side-bars, parallel and connecting rods, gyrating,
    shuttling at thy sides,
Thy metrical, now swelling pant and roar, now tapering in the
    distance,
Thy great protruding head-light fix'd in front,
Thy long, pale, floating vapor-pennants, tinged with delicate
    purple,
The dense and murky clouds out-belching from thy smoke-stack,
Thy knitted frame, thy springs and valves, the tremulous
    twinkle of thy wheels,
Thy train of cars behind, obedient, merrily following,
Through gale or calm, now swift, now slack, yet steadily
    careering;
Type of the modern—emblem of motion and power—pulse of the
    continent,
For once come serve the Muse and merge in verse, even as here
    I see thee,
With storm and buffeting gusts of wind and falling snow,
By day thy warning ringing bell to sound its notes,
By night thy silent signal lamps to swing.

Fierce-throated beauty!
Roll through my chant with all thy lawless music, thy swinging
    lamps at night,
Thy madly-whistled laughter, echoing, rumbling like an
    earthquake, rousing all,
Law of thyself complete, thine own track firmly holding,
(No sweetness debonair of tearful harp or glib piano thine,)
Thy trills of shrieks by rocks and hills return'd,
Launch'd o'er the prairies wide, across the lakes,
To the free skies unpent and glad and strong.

THE DALLIANCE OF THE EAGLES

Skirting the river road, (my forenoon walk, my rest,)
Skyward in air a sudden muffled sound, the dalliance of the eagles,

The rushing amorous contact high in space together,
The clinching interlocking claws, a living, fierce, gyrating
    wheel,
Four beating wings, two beaks, a swirling mass tight grappling,
In tumbling turning clustering loops, straight downward falling,
Till o'er the river pois'd, the twain yet one, a moment's lull,
A motionless still balance in the air, then parting, talons loosing,
Upward again on slow firm pinions slanting, their separate
    diverse flight,
She hers, he his, pursuing.

WITH HUSKY-HAUGHTY LIPS, O SEA!

With husky-haughty lips, O sea!
Where day and night I wend thy surf-beat shore,
Imaging to my sense thy varied strange suggestions,
(I see and plainly list thy talk and conference here,)
Thy troops of white-maned racers racing to the goal,
Thy ample, smiling face, dash'd with the sparkling dimples of the
    sun,
Thy brooding scowl and murk—thy unloos'd hurricanes,
Thy unsubduedness, caprices, wilfulness;
Great as thou art above the rest, thy many tears—a lack from
    all eternity in thy content,
(Naught but the greatest struggles, wrongs, defeats, could make
    thee greatest—no less could make thee,)
Thy lonely state—something thou ever seek'st and seek'st, yet
    never gain'st,
Surely some right withheld—some voice, in huge monotonous
    rage, of freedom-lover pent,
Some vast heart, like a planet's, chain'd and chafing in those
    breakers,
By lengthen'd swell, and spasm, and panting breath,
And rhythmic rasping of thy sands and waves,
And serpent hiss, and savage peals of laughter,
And undertones of distant lion roar,

(Sounding, appealing to the sky's deaf ear—but now, rapport
    for once,
A phantom in the night thy confidant for once,)
The first and last confession of the globe,
Outsurging, muttering from thy soul's abysms,
The tale of cosmic elemental passion,
Thou tellest to a kindred soul.

From "Democratic Vistas"*

Viewed, today, from a point of view sufficiently over-arching, the problem of humanity all over the civilized world is social and religious, and is to be finally met and treated by literature. The priest departs, the divine literatus comes. Never was anything more wanted than, today and here in the States, the poet of the modern is wanted, or the great literatus of the modern. At all times, perhaps, the central point in any nation, and that whence it is itself really swayed the most, and whence it sways others, is its national literature, especially its archetypal poems. Above all previous lands, a great original literature is surely to become the justification and reliance (in some respects the sole reliance,) of American democracy.

Few are aware how the great literature penetrates all, gives hue to all, shapes aggregates and individuals, and, after subtle ways, with irresistible power, constructs, sustains, demolishes at will. Why tower, in reminiscence, above all the nations of the earth, two special lands, petty in themselves, yet inexpressibly gigantic, beautiful, columnar? Immortal Judah lives, and Greece immortal lives, in a couple of poems.

. . . .

In short, as, though it may not be realized, it is strictly true, that a few first-class poets, philosophs, and authors have substantially settled and given status to the entire religion, education, law, sociology, etc., of the hitherto civilized world, by tinge-

---

*Written in 1867–68, revised for book publication in 1871

ing and often creating the atmosphere, out of which they have arisen, such also must stamp, and more than ever stamp, the interior and real democratic construction of this American continent, to-day, and days to come. Remember also this fact of difference, that, while through the antique and through the medieval ages, highest thoughts and ideas realized themselves, and their expression made its way by other arts, as much as, or even more than by, technical literature (not open to the mass of persons, or even to the majority of eminent persons), such literature in our day and for current purposes is not only more eligible than all the other arts put together, but has become the only general means of morally influencing the world. Painting, sculpture, and the dramatic theatre, it would seem, no longer play an indispensable or even important part in the workings and mediumship of intellect, utility, or even high aesthetics. Architecture remains, doubtless with capacities, and a real future. Then music, the combiner, nothing more spiritual, nothing more sensuous, a god, yet completely human, advances, prevails, holds highest place; supplying in certain wants and quarters what nothing else could supply. Yet in the civilization of to-day it is undeniable that, over all the arts, literature dominates, serves beyond all—shapes the character of church and school—or, at any rate, is capable of doing so. Including the literature of science, its scope is indeed unparalleled.

. . . .

The historians say of ancient Greece, with her ever-jealous autonomies, cities, and states, that the only positive unity she ever owned or received, was the sad unity of common subjection, at the last, to foreign conquerors. Subjection, aggregation of that sort, is impossible to America; but the fear of conflicting and irreconcilable interiors, and the lack of a common skeleton, knitting all close, continually haunts me. Or, if it does not, nothing is plainer than the need, a long period to come, of a fusion of the States into the only reliable identity, the moral and artistic one. For, I say, the true nationality of the States, the genuine union, when we come to a mortal crisis, is, and is to be, after all, neither the written law, nor (as is generally supposed) either self-interest, or common pecuniary or material objects—but the fervid and tremendous Idea, melting everything else with resistless heat, and solving all lesser and definite distinctions in vast, indefinite, spiritual, emotional power.

. . . .

But sternly discarding, shutting our eyes to the glow and grandeur of the general superficial effect, coming down to what is of the only real importance, Personalities, and examining minutely, we question, we ask, Are there, indeed, *men* here worthy the name? Are there athletes? Are there perfect women to match the generous material luxuriance? Is there a pervading atmosphere of beautiful manners? Are there crops of fine youths, and majestic old persons? Are there arts worthy freedom and a rich people? Is there a great moral and religious civilization— the only justification of a great material one? Confess that to severe eyes, using the moral microscope upon humanity, a sort of dry and flat Sahara appears, these cities, crowded with petty grotesques, malformations, phantoms, playing meaningless antics. Confess that everywhere, in shops, street, church, theatre, barroom, official chair, are pervading flippancy and vulgarity, low cunning, infidelity—everywhere the youth puny, impudent, foppish, prematurely ripe—everywhere an abnormal libidinousness, unhealthy forms, male, female, painted, padded, dyed, chignoned, muddy complexions, bad blood, the capacity for good motherhood deceasing or deceased, shallow notions of beauty, with a range of manners, or rather lack of manners (considering the advantages enjoyed), probably the meanest to be seen in the world.

. . . .

Of all this, and these lamentable conditions, to breathe into them the breath recuperative of sane and heroic life, I say a new-founded literature, not merely to copy and reflect existing surfaces, or pander to what is called taste—not only to amuse, pass away time, celebrate the beautiful, the refined, the past, or exhibit technical, rhythmic, or grammatical dexterity—but a literature underlying life, religious, consistent with science, handling the elements and forces with competent power, teaching and training men—and, as perhaps the most precious of its results, achieving the entire redemption of woman out of these incredible holds and webs of silliness, millinery, and every kind of dyspeptic depletion—and thus insuring to the States a strong and sweet Female Race, a race of perfect Mothers—is what is needed.

And now, in the full conception of these facts, and points, and all that they infer, pro and con—with yet unshaken faith in the elements of the American masses, the composites, of both sexes, and even considered as individuals—and ever recognizing in them the broadest bases of the best literary and aesthetic appreciation—I proceed with my speculations, Vistas.
. . . .

The purpose of democracy—supplanting old belief in the necessary absoluteness of established dynastic rulership, temporal, ecclesiastical, and scholastic as furnishing the only security against chaos, crime, and ignorance—is, through many transmigrations and amid endless ridicules, arguments, and ostensible failures, to illustrate, at all hazards, this doctrine or theory that man, properly trained in sanest, highest freedom, may and must become a law, and series of laws, unto himself, surrounding and providing for, not only his own personal control, but all his relations to other individuals, and to the State; and that, while other theories, as in the past histories of nations, have proved wise enough, and indispensable perhaps for their conditions, *this,* as matters now stand in our civilized world, is the only scheme worth working from, as warranting results like those of Nature's laws, reliable, when once established, to carry on themselves.
. . . .

Political democracy, as it exists and practically works in America, with all its threatening evils, supplies a training-school for making first-class men. It is life's gymnasium, not of good only, but of all. We try often, though we fall back often. A brave delight, fit for freedom's athletes, fills these arenas, and fully satisfies, out of the action in them, irrespective of success. Whatever we do not attain, we at any rate attain the experiences of the fight, the hardening of the strong campaign, and throb with currents of attempt at least. Time is ample. Let the victors come after us. Not for nothing does evil play its part among us. Judging from the main portions of the history of the world, so far, justice is always in jeopardy, peace walks amid hourly pitfalls, and of slavery, misery, meanness, the craft of tyrants and the credulity of the populace, in some of their protean forms, no voice can at any time say, They are not. The clouds break a little, and the sun shines out—but soon and certain the lowering darkness falls again, as if to last forever. Yet is there an immortal courage and prophecy in every sane soul that cannot, must not, under any circumstances, capitulate. *Vive*, the attack—the perennial assault! *Vive*, the unpopular cause—the spirit that audaciously aims— the never-abandoned efforts, pursued the same amid opposing proofs and precedents.

. . . .

Democracy, in silence, biding its time, ponders its own ideals, not of literature and art only—not of men only, but of women. The idea of the women of America (extricated from this daze, this fossil and unhealthy air which hangs about the word *lady*) developed, raised to become the robust equals, workers, and, it may be, even practical and political deciders with the men— greater than man, we may admit, through their divine maternity, always their towering, emblematical attribute—but great, at any rate, as man, in all departments; or rather, capable of being so, soon as they realize it, and can bring themselves to give up toys and fictions, and launch forth, as men do, amid real, independent, stormy life.

Then, as toward our thought's finale, (and, in that, over-arching the true scholar's lesson,) we have to say there can be no complete or epical presentation of democracy in the aggregate, or anything like it, at this day, because its doctrines will only be effectually incarnated in any one branch, when, in all, their spirit is at the root and center. Far, far, indeed, stretch, in distance, our Vistas! How much is still to be disentangled, freed! How long it takes to make this American world see that it is, in itself, the final authority and reliance!

Did you, too, O friend, suppose democracy was only for elections, for politics, and for a party name? I say democracy is only of use there that it may pass on and come to its flower and fruits in manners, in the highest forms of interaction between men, and their beliefs—in religion, literature, colleges, and schools —democracy in all public and private life, and in the army and navy. I have intimated that, as a paramount scheme, it has yet few or no full realizers and believers. I do not see, either, that it owes any serious thanks to noted propagandists or champions, or has been essentially helped, though often harmed, by them. It has been and is carried on by all the moral forces, and by trade, finance, machinery, intercommunications, and, in fact, by all the developments of history, and can no more be stopped than the tides, or the earth in its orbit. Doubtless, also, it resides, crude and latent, well down in the hearts of the fair average of the American-born people, mainly in the agricultural regions. But it is not yet, there or anywhere, the fully received, the fervid, the absolute faith.

. . . .

And, if we think of it, what does civilization itself rest upon— and what object has it, what its religions, arts, schools, etc., but rich, luxuriant, varied personalism? To that, all bends; and it is because toward such result democracy alone, on anything like Nature's scale, breaks up the limitless fallows of human-kind, and plants the seed, and gives fair play, that its claims now precede the rest. The literature, songs, aesthetics, etc., of a country are of importance principally because they furnish the materials and suggestions of personality for the women and men of that country, and enforce them in a thousand effective ways. As the topmost claim of a strong consolidating of the nationality of these States is, that only by such powerful compaction can the separate States secure that full and free swing within their spheres, which is becoming to them, each after its kind, so will individuality, and unimpeded branchings, flourish best under imperial republican forms.

. . . .

In the prophetic literature of these States (the reader of my speculations will miss their principal stress unless he allows well for the point that a new Literature, perhaps a new Metaphysics, certainly a new Poetry, are to be, in my opinion, the only sure and worthy supports and expressions of the American Democracy,) Nature, true Nature, and the true idea of Nature, long absent, must, above all, become fully restored, enlarged, and must furnish the pervading atmosphere to poems, and the test of all high literary and aesthetic compositions. I do not mean the smooth walks, trimmed hedges, posys and nightingales of the English poets, but the whole orb, with its geologic history, the kosmos, carrying fire and snow, that rolls through the illimitable areas, light as a feather, though weighing billions of tons. Furthermore, as by what we now partially call Nature is intended, at most, only what is entertainable by the physical conscience, the sense of matter, and of good animal health—on these it must be distinctly accumulated, incorporated, that man, comprehending these, has, in towering superaddition, the moral and spiritual consciences, indicating his destination beyond the ostensible, the mortal.

. . . .

We see, as in the universes of the material kosmos, after meteorological, vegetable, and animal cycles, man at last arises, born through them, to prove them, concentrate them, to turn upon them with wonder and love—to command them, adorn them, and carry them upward into superior realms—so, out of the series of the preceding social and political universes, now arise these States. We see that while many were supposing things established and completed, really the grandest things always remain; and discover that the work of the New World is not ended, but only fairly begun.

We see our land, America, her literature, aesthetics, etc., as, substantially, the getting in form, or effusement and statement, of deepest basic elements and loftiest final meanings, of history and man—and the portrayal (under the eternal laws and conditions of beauty,) of our own physiognomy, the subjective tie and expression of the objective, as from our own combination, continuation, and points of view—and the deposit and record of the national mentality, character, appeals, heroism, wars, and even liberties—where these, and all, culminate in native literary and artistic formulation, to be perpetuated; and not having which native, first-class formulation, she will flounder about, and her other, however imposing, eminent greatness, prove merely a passing gleam; but truly having which, she will understand herself, live nobly, nobly contribute, emanate, and swinging, poised safely on herself, illumined and illuming, become a full-formed world, and divine Mother not only of material but spiritual worlds, in ceaseless succession through time—the main thing being the average, the bodily, the concrete, the democratic, the popular, on which all the superstructures of the future are to permanently rest.

From "Specimen Days"

DOWN AT THE FRONT

Falmouth, Va., opposite Fredericksburgh, December 21, 1862.
Begin my visits among the camp hospitals in the army of the
Potomac. Spend a good part of the day in a large brick mansion
on the banks of the Rappahannock, used as a hospital since the
battle—seems to have receiv'd only the worst cases. Out doors,
at the foot of a tree, within ten yards of the front of the house,
I noticed a heap of amputated feet, legs, arms, hands, etc., a full
load for a one-horse cart. Several dead bodies lie near, each
cover'd with its brown woollen blanket. In the door-yard,
towards the river, are fresh graves mostly of officers, their names
on pieces of barrel staves or broken boards, stuck in the dirt.
(Most of these bodies were subsequently taken up and transported north to their friends.) The large mansion is quite
crowded upstairs and down, everything impromptu, no system,
all bad enough, but I have no doubt the best that can be done; all
wounds pretty bad, some frightful, the men in their old clothes,
unclean and bloody. Some of the wounded are rebel soldiers and
officers, prisoners. One, a Mississippian, a captain, hit badly in leg,
I talk'd with some time; he ask'd me for papers, which I gave him.
(I saw him three months afterward in Washington, with his leg
amputated, doing well.) I went through the rooms, downstairs
and up. Some of the men were dying. I had nothing to give at that
visit, but wrote a few letters to folks home, mothers, etc. Also
talk'd to three or four, who seem'd most susceptible to it, and
needing it.

198

AFTER FIRST FREDERICKSBURG

December 23 to 31. The results of the late battle are exhibited everywhere about here in thousands of cases, (hundreds die every day,) in the camp, brigade, and division hospitals. These are merely tents, and sometimes very poor ones, the wounded lying on the ground, lucky if their blankets are spread on layers of pine or hemlock twigs, or small leaves. No cots; seldom even a mattress. It is pretty cold. The ground is frozen hard, and there is occasional snow. I go around from one case to another. I do not see that I do much good to these wounded and dying; but I cannot leave them. Once in a while some youngster holds on to me convulsively, and I do what I can for him; at any rate, stop with him and sit near him for hours, if he wishes it.

Besides the hospitals, I also go occasionally on long tours through the camps, talking with the men, etc. Sometimes at night among the groups around the fires, in their shebang enclosures of bushes. These are curious shows, full of characters and groups. I soon get acquainted anywhere in camp, with officers or men, and am always well used. Sometimes I go down on picket with the regiments I know best. As to rations, the army here at present seems to be tolerably well supplied, and the men have enough, such as it is, mainly salt pork and hard tack. Most of the regiments lodge in the flimsy little shelter-tents. A few have built themselves huts of logs and mud, with fireplaces.

BACK TO WASHINGTON

January, '63. Left camp at Falmouth, with some wounded, a few days since, and came here by Aquia creek railroad, and so on government steamer up the Potomac. Many wounded were with us on the cars and boat. The cars were just common platform ones. The railroad journey of ten or twelve miles was made mostly before sunrise. The soldiers guarding the road came out from their tents or shebangs of bushes with rumpled hair and half-awake look. Those on duty were walking their posts, some on banks over us, others down far below the level of the track. I saw large cavalry camps off the road. At Aquia creek landing were numbers of wounded going north. While I waited some three hours, I went around among them. Several wanted word sent home to parents, brothers, wives, etc., which I did for them, (by mail the next day from Washington). On the boat I had my hands full. One poor fellow died going up.

Thursday, Jan. 21. Devoted the main part of the day to Armory square hospital; went pretty thoroughly through wards F, G, H, and I; some fifty cases in each ward. In ward F supplied the men throughout with writing paper and stamp'd envelope each; distributed in small portions, to proper subjects, a large jar of first-rate preserv'd berries, which had been donated to me by a lady— her own cooking. Found several cases I thought good subjects for small sums of money, which I furnish'd. (The wounded men often come up broke, and it helps their spirits to have even the small sum I give them.) My paper and envelopes all gone, but distributed a good lot of amusing reading matter; also, as I thought judicious, tobacco, oranges, apples, etc. Interesting cases in ward I; Charles Miller, bed 19, company D, 53rd Pennsylvania, is only sixteen years of age, very bright, courageous boy, left leg amputated below the knee; next bed to him, another young lad very sick; gave each appropriate gifts. In the bed above also, amputation of the left leg; gave him a little jar of raspberries; bed 1, this ward, gave a small sum; also to a soldier on crutches, sitting on his bed near. (I am more and more surprised at the very great proportion of youngsters from fifteen to twenty-one in the army. I afterwards found a still greater proportion among the southerners.)

Evening, same day, went to see D. F. R., before alluded to; found him remarkably changed for the better; up and dress'd— quite a triumph; he afterwards got well, and went back to his regiment. Distributed in the wards a quantity of notepaper, and forty or fifty stamp'd envelopes, of which I had recruited my stock, and the men were much in need.

ABRAHAM LINCOLN

August 12 [*1863*]. I see the President almost every day, as I happen to live where he passes to or from his lodgings out of town. He never sleeps at the White House during the hot season, but has quarters at a healthy location some three miles north of the city, the Soldiers' Home, a United States military establishment. I saw him this morning about 8½ coming in to business, riding on Vermont avenue, near L street. He always has a company of twenty-five or thirty cavalry, with sabers drawn and held upright over their shoulders. They say this guard was against his personal wish, but he let his counselors have their way. The party makes no great show in uniform or horses. Mr. Lincoln on the saddle generally rides a good-sized, easy-going gray horse, is dress'd in plain black, somewhat rusty and dusty, wears a black stiff hat, and looks about as ordinary in attire, etc., as the commonest man. A lieutenant, with yellow straps, rides at his left, and following behind, two by two, come the cavalry men, in their yellow-striped jackets. They are generally going at a slow trot, as that is the pace set them by the one they wait upon. The sabers and accouterments clank, and the entirely unornamental *cortège* as it trots toward Lafayette square arouses no sensation, only some curious stranger stops and gazes. I see very plainly Abraham Lincoln's dark brown face, with the deep-cut lines, the eyes, always to me with a deep latent sadness in the expression. We have got so that we exchange bows, and very cordial ones. Sometimes the President goes and comes in an open barouche. The cavalry always accompany him, with drawn sabers. Often I notice as he goes out evenings—and sometimes in the morning, when he returns early—he turns off and halts at the large and handsome residence of the Secretary of War, on K street, and holds conference there. If in his barouche, I can see from my window he does not alight, but sits in his vehicle, and Mr. Stanton comes out to attend him. Sometimes one of his sons, a boy of ten or twelve, accompanies him, riding at his right on a pony. Earlier in the summer I occasionally saw the President and his wife, toward the latter part of the afternoon, out in a barouche, on a pleasure ride through the city. Mrs. Lincoln was dress'd in complete black, with a long crape veil. The equipage is of the plainest kind, only two horses, and they nothing extra. They pass'd me once very close, and I saw the President in the face fully, as they were moving slowly, and his look, though abstracted, happen'd to be directed steadily in my eye. He bow'd and smiled, but far beneath his smile I noticed well the expression I have alluded to. None of the artists or pictures has caught the deep, though subtle and indirect expression of this man's face. There is something else there. One of the great portrait painters of two or three centuries ago is needed.

VIRGINIA

Dilapidated, fenceless, and trodden with war as Virginia is, wherever I move across her surface, I find myself rous'd to surprise and admiration. What capacity for products, improvements, human life, nourishment and expansion. Everywhere that I have been in the old Dominion, (the subtle mockery of that title now!) such thoughts have fill'd me. The soil is yet far above the average of any of the northern States: And how full of breadth the scenery, everywhere distant mountains, everywhere convenient rivers. Even yet prodigal in forest woods, and surely eligible for all the fruits, orchards, and flowers. The skies and atmosphere most luscious, as I feel certain, from more than a year's residence in the State, and movements hither and yon. I should say very healthy, as a general thing. Then a rich and elastic quality, by night and by day. The sun rejoices in his strength, dazzling and burning, and yet, to me, never unpleasantly weakening. It is not the panting tropical heat, but invigorates. The north tempers it. The nights are often unsurpassable. Last evening (Feb. 8,) I saw the first of the new moon, the outlined old moon clear along with it; the sky and air so clear, such transparent hues of color, it seem'd to me I had never really seen the new moon before. It was the thinnest cut crescent possible. It hung delicate just above the sulky shadow of the Blue mountains. Ah, if it might prove an omen and good prophecy for this unhappy State.

THE INAUGURATION

March 4 [*1865*]. The President very quietly rode down to the capitol in his own carriage, by himself, on a sharp trot, about noon, either because he wish'd to be on hand to sign bills, or to get rid of marching in line with the absurd procession, the muslin temple of liberty, and pasteboard monitor. I saw him on his return, at three o'clock, after the performance was over. He was in his plain two-horse barouche, and look'd very much worn and tired; the lines, indeed, of vast responsibilities, intricate questions, and demands of life and death, cut deeper than ever upon his dark brown face; yet all the old goodness, tenderness, sadness, and canny shrewdness, underneath the furrows. (I never see that man without feeling that he is one to become personally attach'd to, for his combination of purest, heartiest tenderness, and native western form of manliness.) By his side sat his little boy, of ten years. There were no soldiers, only a lot of civilians on horseback, with huge yellow scarfs over their shoulders, riding around the carriage. (At the inauguration four years ago, he rode down and back again surrounded by a dense mass of arm'd cavalrymen eight deep, with drawn sabers; and there were sharp-shooters station'd at every corner on the route.) I ought to make mention of the closing levee of Saturday night last. Never before was such a compact jam in front of the White House—all the grounds fill'd, and away out to the spacious sidewalks. I was there, as I took a notion to go—was in the rush inside with the crowd—surged along the passage-ways, the blue and other rooms, and through the great east room. Crowds of country people, some very funny. Fine music from the Marine band, off in a side place. I saw Mr. Lincoln, drest all in black, with white kid gloves and a claw-hammer coat, receiving, as in duty bound, shaking hands, looking very disconsolate, and as if he would give anything to be somewhere else.

INAUGURATION BALL

March 6. I have been up to look at the dance and supper rooms, for the inauguration ball at the Patent Office; and I could not help thinking, what a different scene they presented to my view a while since, fill'd with a crowded mass of the worst wounded of the war, brought in from second Bull Run, Antietam, and Fredericksburgh. To-night, beautiful women, perfumes, the violins' sweetness, the polka and the waltz; then the amputation, the blue face, the groan, the glassy eye of the dying, the clotted rag, the odor of wounds and blood, and many a mother's son amid strangers, passing away untended there, (for the crowd of the badly hurt was great, and much for nurse to do, and much for surgeon).

SCENE AT THE CAPITOL

I must mention a strange scene at the capitol, the Hall of Representatives, the morning of Saturday last (March 4). The day just dawn'd, but in half-darkness, everything dim, leaden, and soaking. In that dim light, the members nervous from long drawn duty, exhausted, some asleep, and many half asleep. The gaslight, mix'd with the dingy daybreak, produced an unearthly effect. The poor little sleepy, stumbling pages, the smell of the hall, the members with heads leaning on their desks, the sounds of the voices speaking, with unusual intonations—the general moral atmosphere also of the close of this important session—the strong hope that the war is approaching its close—the tantalizing dread lest the hope may be a false one—the grandeur of the hall itself, with its effect of vast shadows up toward the panels and spaces over the galleries—all made a mark'd combination.

In the midst of this, with the suddenness of a thunderbolt, burst one of the most angry and crashing storms of rain and hail ever heard. It beat like a deluge on the heavy glass roof of the hall, and the wind literally howl'd and roar'd. For a moment, (and no wonder,) the nervous and sleeping Representatives were thrown into confusion. The slumberers awaked with fear, some started for the doors, some look'd up with blanch'd cheeks and lips to the roof, and the little pages began to cry; it was a scene. But it was over almost as soon as the drowsied men were actually awake. They recover'd themselves; the storm raged on, beating, dashing, and with loud noises at times. But the House went ahead with its business then, I think, as calmly and with as much deliberation as at any time in its career. Perhaps the shock did it good. (One is not without impression, after all, amid these members of Congress, of both the Houses, that if the flat routine of their duties should ever be broken in upon by some great emergency involving real danger, and calling for first-class personal qualities, those qualities would be found generally forthcoming, and from men not now credited with them.)

THE REAL WAR WILL NEVER GET IN THE BOOKS

And so good-by to the war. I know not how it may have been, or may be, to others—to me the main interest I found, (and still, on recollection, find,) in the rank and file of the armies, both sides, and in those specimens amid the hospitals, and even the dead on the field. To me the points illustrating the latent personal character and eligibilities of these States, in the two or three million of American young and middle-aged men, North and South, embodied in those armies—and especially the one-third or one-fourth of their number, stricken by wounds or disease at some time in the course of the contest—were of more significence even than the political interest involved. (And so much of a race depends on how it faces death, and how it stands personal anguish and sickness. As, in the glints of emotions under emergencies, and the indirect traits and asides in Plutarch, we get far profounder clues to the antique world than all its more formal history.)

Future years will never know the seething hell and the black infernal background of countless minor scenes and interiors, (not the official surface-courteousness of the Generals, not the few great battles) of the Secession War; and it is best they should not—the real war will never get in the books. In the mushy influences of current times, too, the fervid atmosphere and typical events of those years are in danger of being totally forgotten. I have at night watch'd by the side of a sick man in the hospital, one who could not live many hours. I have seen his eyes flash and burn as he raised himself and recurr'd to the cruelties on his surrender'd brother, and mutilations of the corpse afterward. (See, in the preceding pages, the incident at Upperville—the seventeen kill'd as in the description, were left there on the ground. After they dropt dead, no one touch'd them—all were made sure of, however. The carcasses were left for the citizens to bury or not, as they chose.)

Such was the war. It was not a quadrille in a ballroom. Its interior history will not only never be written—its practicality, minutiae of deeds and passions will never be even suggested. The actual soldier of 1862-'65, North and South, with all his ways, his incredible dauntlessness, habits, practices, tastes, language, his fierce friendship, his appetite, rankness, his superb strength and animality, lawless gait, and a hundred unnamed lights and shades of camp, I say, will never be written—perhaps must not and should not be. . . .

NEW THEMES ENTERED UPON

1876-77. I find the woods in mid-May and early June my best places for composition. Seated on logs or stumps there, or resting on rails, nearly all the following memoranda have been jotted down. Wherever I go, indeed, winter or summer, city or country, alone at home or traveling. I must take notes —(the ruling passion strong in age and disablement, and even the approach of —but I must not say it yet). Then underneath the following excerpta—crossing the *t's* and dotting the *i's* of certain moderate movements of late years—I am fain to fancy the foundations of quite a lesson learn'd. After you have exhausted what there is in business, politics, conviviality, love, and so on—have found that none of these finally satisfy, or permanently wear—what remains? Nature remains; to bring out from their torpid recesses, the affinities of a man or woman with the open air, the trees, fields, the changes of seasons—the sun by day and the stars of heaven by night. We will begin from these convictions. Literature flies so high and is so hotly spiced, that our notes may seem hardly more than breaths of common air, or draughts of water to drink. But that is part of our lesson.

Dear, soothing, healthy, restoration-hours—after three confining years of paralysis—after the long strain of the war, and its wounds and death.

ENTERING A LONG FARM LANE

As every man has his hobby-liking, mine is for a real farm lane fenced by old chestnut-rails gray-green with dabs of moss and lichen, copious weeds and briers growing in spots athwart the heaps of stray-pick'd stones at the fence bases—irregular paths worn between, and horse and cow tracks—all characteristic accompaniments marking and scenting the neighborhood in their seasons—apple tree blossoms in forward April—pigs, poultry, a field of August buckwheat, and in another the long flapping tassels of maize—and so to the pond, the expansion of the creek, the secluded-beautiful, with young and old trees, and such recesses and vistas.

A JULY AFTERNOON BY THE POND

The fervent heat, but so much more endurable in this pure air—the white and pink pond-blossoms, with great heart-shaped leaves; the glassy waters of the creek, the banks, with dense bushery, and the picturesque beeches and shade and turf; the tremulous, reedy call of some bird from recesses, breaking the warm, indolent, half-voluptuous silence; an occasional wasp, hornet, honey-bee or bumble (they hover near my hands or face, yet annoy me not, nor I them, as they appear to examine, find nothing, and away they go)—the vast space of the sky overhead so clear, and the buzzard up there sailing his slow whirl in majestic spirals and discs; just over the surface of the pond, two large slate-color'd dragon-flies, with wings of lace, circling and darting and occasionally balancing themselves quite still, their wings quivering all the time, (are they not showing off for my amusement?)— the pond itself, with the sword-shaped calamus; the water snakes —occasionally a flitting blackbird, with red dabs on his shoulders, as he darts slantingly by—the sounds that bring out the solitude, warmth, light and shade—the quawk of some pond duck—(the crickets and grasshoppers are mute in the noon heat, but I hear the song of the first cicadas;)—then at some distance the rattle and whirr of a reaping machine as the horses draw it on a rapid walk through a rye field on the opposite side of the creek— (what was the yellow or light-brown bird, large as a young hen, with short neck and long-stretch'd legs I just saw, in flapping and awkward flight over there through the trees?)—the prevailing delicate, yet palpable, spicy, grassy, clovery perfume to my nostrils; and over all, encircling all, to my sight and soul, the free space of the sky, transparent and blue—and hovering there in the west, a mass of white-gray fleecy clouds the sailors call "shoals of mackerel"—the sky, with silver swirls like locks of toss'd hair, spreading, expanding—a vast voiceless, formless simulacrum—yet maybe the most real reality and formulator of everything—who knows?

THE SKY—DAYS AND NIGHTS—HAPPINESS

Oct. 20. A clear, crispy day—dry and breezy air, full of oxygen. Out of the same, silent, beauteous miracles that envelop and fuse me—trees, water, grass, sunlight, and early frost—the one I am looking at most today is the sky. It has that delicate, transparent blue, peculiar to autumn, and the only clouds are little or larger white ones, giving their still and spiritual motion to the great concave. All through the earlier day (say from 7 to 11) it keeps a pure, yet vivid blue. But as noon approaches the color gets lighter, quite gray for two or three hours—then still paler for a spell, till sun-down—which last I watch dazzling through the interstices of a knoll of big trees—darts of fire and a gorgeous show of light-yellow, liver-color and red, with a vast silver glaze askant on the water—the transparent shadows, shafts, sparkle, and vivid colors beyond all the paintings ever made.

I don't know what or how, but it seems to me mostly owing to these skies, (every now and then I think, while I have of course seen them every day of my life, I never really saw the skies before,) I have had this autumn some wondrously contented hours —may I not say perfectly happy ones? As I've read, Byron just before his death told a friend that he had known but three happy hours during his whole existence. Then there is the old German legend of the king's bell, to the same point. While I was out there by the wood, that beautiful sunset through the trees, I thought of Byron's and the bell story, and the notion started in me that I was having a happy hour. (Though perhaps my best moments I never jot down; when they come I cannot afford to break the charm by inditing memoranda. I just abandon myself to the mood, and let it float on, carrying me in its placid extasy.)

What is happiness, anyhow? Is this one of its hours, or the like of it?—so impalpable—a mere breath, an evanescent tinge? I am not sure—so let me give myself the benefit of the doubt. Hast Thou, pellucid, in Thy azure depths, medicine for case like mine? (Ah, the physical shatter and troubled spirit of me the last three years!) And dost Thou subtly, mystically now drip it through the air invisibly upon me?

SEASHORE FANCIES

Even as a boy, I had the fancy, the wish, to write a piece, perhaps a poem, about the sea-shore—that suggesting, dividing line, contact, junction, the solid marrying the liquid—that curious, lurking something, (as doubtless every objective form finally becomes to the subjective spirit,) which means far more than its mere first sight, grand as that is—blending the real and ideal, and each made portion of the other. Hours, days, in my Long Island youth and early manhood, I haunted the shores of Rockaway or Coney island, or away east to the Hamptons or Montauk. Once, at the latter place, (by the old lighthouse, nothing but sea-tossings in sight in every direction as far as the eye could reach,) I remember well, I felt that I must one day write a book expressing this liquid, mystic theme. Afterward, I recollect, how it came to me that instead of any special lyrical or epical or literary attempt the sea-shore should be an invisible *influence*, a pervading gauge and tally for me, in my composition. (Let me give a hint here to young writers. I am not sure but I have unwittingly follow'd out the same rule with other powers besides sea and shores—avoiding them, in the way of any dead set at poetizing them, as too big for formal handling—quite satisfied if I could indirectly show that we have met and fused, even if only once, but enough—that we have really absorb'd each other and understand each other.)

There is a dream, a picture, that for years at intervals, (sometimes quite long ones, but surely again, in time,) has come noiselessly up before me, and I really believe, fiction as it is, has enter'd largely into my practical life—certainly into my writings, and shaped and color'd them. It is nothing more or less than a stretch of interminable white-brown sand, hard and smooth and broad, with the ocean perpetually, grandly, rolling in upon it, with slow-measured sweep, with rustle and hiss and foam, and many a thump as of low bass drums. This scene, this picture, I say, has risen before me at times for years. Sometimes I wake at night and can hear and see it plainly.

FULL-STARR'D NIGHTS

May 21. Back in Camden. Again commencing one of those unusually transparent, full-starr'd blue-black nights as if to show that however lush and pompous the day may be, there is something left in the not-day that can outvie it. The rarest, finest sample of long-drawnout clear-obscure, from sundown to 9 o'clock. I went down to the Delaware, and cross'd and cross'd. Venus like blazing silver well up in the west. The large pale thin crescent of the new moon, half an hour high, sinking languidly under a bar-sinister of cloud, and then emerging. Arcturus right overhead. A faint fragrant sea-odor wafted up from the south. The gloaming, the temper'd coolness, with every feature of the scene, indescribably soothing and tonic—one of those hours that gives hints to the soul, impossible to put in a statement. (Ah, where would be any food for spirituality without night and the stars?) The vacant spaciousness of the air, and the veil'd blue of the heavens, seem'd miracles enough.

As the night advanc'd it changed its spirit and garments to ampler stateliness. I was almost conscious of a definite presence, Nature silently near. The great constellation of the Water-Serpent stretch'd its coils over more than half the heavens. The Swan with outspread wings was flying down the Milky Way. The northern Crown, the Eagle, Lyra, all up there in their places. From the whole dome shot down points of light, rapport with me, through the clear blue-black. All the usual sense of motion, all animal life, seem'd discarded, seem'd a fiction; a curious power, like the placid rest of Egyptian gods, took possession, none the less potent for being impalpable. Earlier I had seen many bats, balancing in the luminous twilight, darting their black forms hither and yon over the river; but now they altogether disappear'd. The evening star and the moon had gone. Alertness and peace lay calmly couching together through the fluid universal shadows.

August 26. Bright has the day been, and my spirits an equal *forzando.* Then comes the night, different, inexpressibly pensive, with its own tender and temper'd splendor. Venus lingers in the west with a voluptuous dazzle unshown hitherto this summer. Mars rises early, and the red sulky moon, two days past her full; Jupiter at night's meridian, and the long curling-slanted Scorpion stretching full view in the south, Aretus-neck'd. Mars walks the heavens lord-paramount now; all through this month I go out after supper and watch for him; sometimes getting up at midnight to take another look at his unparallel'd lustre. (I see lately an

astronomer has made out through the new Washington tele-
scope that Mars has certainly one moon, perhaps two.) Pale and
distant, but near in the heavens, Saturn precedes him.

MULLEINS AND MULLEINS

Large, placid mulleins, as summer advances, velvety in texture,
of a light greenish-drab color, growing everywhere in the fields
—at first earth's big rosettes in their broad-leav'd low cluster-
plants, eight, ten, twenty leaves to a plant—plentiful on the
fallow twenty-acre lot, at the end of the lane, and especially
by the ridge-sides of the fences—then close to the ground, but
soon springing up—leaves as broad as my hand, and the lower
ones twice as long—so fresh and dewy in the morning—stalks
now four or five, even seven or eight feet high. The farmers, I
find, think the mullein a mean, unworthy weed, but I have grown
to a fondness for it. Every object has its lesson, enclosing the
suggestion of everything else—and lately I sometimes think all
is concentrated for me in these hardy, yellow-flower'd weeds.
As I come down the lane early in the morning, I pause before
their soft wool-like fleece and stem and broad leaves, glittering
with countleess diamonds. Annually for three summers now,
they and I have silently return'd together; at such long intervals
I stand or sit among them, musing—and woven with the rest,
of so many hours and moods of partial rehabilitation—of my sane
or sick spirit, here as near at peace as it can be.

A SUN BATH—NAKEDNESS

Sunday, Aug. 27, [*1877*]. Another day quite free from mark'd
prostration and pain. It seems indeed as if peace and nutriment
from heaven subtly filter into me as I slowly hobble down these
country lanes and across fields, in the good air—as I sit here
in solitude with Nature—open, voiceless, mystic, far removed,
yet palpable, eloquent Nature. I merge myself in the scene, in
the perfect day. Hovering over the clear brook-water, I am

sooth'd by its soft gurgle in one place, and the hoarser murmurs of its three-foot fall in another. Come, ye disconsolate, in whom any latent eligibility is left—come get the sure virtues of creek-shore, and wood and field. Two months (July and August, '77,) have I absorb'd them, and they begin to make a new man of me. Every day, seclusion—every day at least two or three hours of freedom, bathing, no talk, no bonds, no dress, no books, no *manners*.

Shall I tell you, reader, to what I attribute my already much-restored health? That I have been almost two years, off and on, without drugs and medicines, and daily in the open air. Last summer I found a particularly secluded little dell off one side by my creek, originally a large dug-out marl-pit, now abandon'd, fill'd with bushes, trees, grass, a group of willows, a straggling bank, and a spring of delicious water running right through the middle of it, with two or three little cascades. Here I retreated every hot day, and follow it up this summer. Here I realize the meaning of that old fellow who said he was seldom less alone than when alone. Never before did I get so close to Nature; never before did she come so close to me. By old habit, I pencil'd down, from time to time, almost automatically, moods, sights, hours, tints and outlines, on the spot. Let me specially record the satisfaction of this current forenoon, so serene and primitive, so conventionally exceptional, natural.

An hour or so after breakfast I wended my way down to the recesses of the aforesaid dell, which I and certain thrushes, cat-birds, etc., had all to ourselves. A light southwest wind was blowing through the tree-tops. It was just the place and time for my Adamic air-bath and flesh-brushing from head to foot. So hanging clothes on a rail near by, keeping old broad-brim straw on head and easy shoes on feet, haven't I had a good time the last two hours! First with the stiff-elastic bristles rasping arms, breast, sides, till they turn'd scarlet—then partially bathing in the clear waters of the running brook—taking everything very leisurely, with many rests and pauses—stepping about barefooted every few minutes now and then in some neighboring black ooze, for unctuous mudbath to my feet—a brief second and third rinsing in the crystal running waters—rubbing with the fragrant towel—slow, negligent promenades on the turf up and down in the sun, varied with occasional rests, and further frictions of the bristle-brush—sometimes carrying my portable chair with me from place to place, as my range is quite extensive here, nearly a hundred rods, feeling quite secure from intrusion, (and that indeed I am not at all nervous about, if it accidentally happens).

As I walk'd slowly over the grass, the sun shone out enough to show the shadow moving with me. Somehow I seem'd to get identity with each and everything around me, in its condition. Nature was naked, and I was also. It was too lazy, soothing, and joyous-equable to speculate about. Yet I might have thought somehow in this vein: Perhaps the inner never-lost rapport we hold with earth, light, air, trees, etc., is not to be realized through eyes and mind only, but through the whole corporeal body, which I will not have blinded or bandaged any more than the eyes. Sweet, sane, still Nakedness in Nature!—ah if poor, sick, prurient humanity in cities might really know you once more! Is not nakedness then indecent? No, not inherently. It is your thought, your sophistication, your fear, your respectability, that is indecent. There come moods when these clothes of ours are not only too irksome to wear, but are themselves indecent. Perhaps indeed he or she to whom the free exhilarating extasy of nakedness in Nature has never been eligible (and how many thousands there are!) has not really known what purity is—nor what faith or art or health really is. (Probably the whole curriculum of first-class philosophy, beauty, heroism, form, illustrated by the old Hellenic race—the highest height and deepest depth known to civilization in those departments—came from their natural and religious idea of Nakedness.)

Many such hours, from time to time, the last two summers—I attribute my partial rehabilitation largely to them. Some good people may think it a feeble or half-crack'd way of spending one's time and thinking. Maybe it is.

SELECTED CRITICISM

Walt Whitman's Career

. . . In the passing away of a writer whom his admirers loved to call the Good Gray Poet the City of New York has lost the most remarkable literary character since Washington Irving. If his merits are not conceded so generally as are those of Irving, it may be said that his was much the more singular character and career, and that while Irving followed close on English precedents in prose literature, Whitman struck out a path for himself in verse. As to originality, Poe is his only rival. Both formed other writers. Poe left his mark on Frenchmen like Baudelaire and Scotchmen like Robert Louis Stevenson. Whitman had the honor of causing Alfred Lord Tennyson to change his style late in life, as appears from the Jubilee Ode published in honor of Queen Victoria in 1887. Among those of little note whom he influenced was the unfortunate Ada Isaacs Menken, whose slender volume of verse is full of Whitmanisms.

Whitman was a New York poet in more ways than one. His ancestry was half Dutch, half English; his birthplace Long Island; his home for many years alternately Brooklyn or New York, and his heart at all times was centered on our great, vibrating hive of a city. But New York never cared for Walt Whitman or bought his books or read them.

. . . Nor did Whitman confine himself to a theoretical egotism in his writings, but liked the incense of public recognition so well

From obituary in the *New York Times*, Sunday, March 27, 1892, p. 10, columns 1–3, unsigned.

that his dress and behavior on the street often appeared to be calculated to insure conspicuousness, but, as we have seen, this petty vanity was apparent rather than actual. In his intercourse with men and women he impressed his own personality at all times, often rousing great affection, and in many cases lifelong friendships resulted long before he reached that mellow patriarchal stage with which the present generation is familiar.

His odd dress—wide open flannel shirt, wide trousers, broad-brimmed soft hat, and thick stick—prejudiced against him many persons who thought that he was merely a vain fellow who sought notoriety at any cost. Many, also, who took the trouble to read his verse were repelled by the apparent lawlessness of versification and the tremendous heaping up of epithets, repetitions, and eccentric grammar. And of those who condoned or enjoyed these oddities a goodly part fell away when they came to read the passages in which Whitman contends like an inspired physiologist for the beauty and dignity, nay, the poetry of functions and organs not mentioned save in medical works.

Whitman's great strength and his great weakness was generalization. He strikes it in the first lines of "Leaves of Grass":

> *One's self I sing—a simple, separate person;*
> *Yet utter the word Democratic, the word En masse,*

and is at pains to talk often of the 'ensemble' and to use other French words (ma femme, feuillage, repondez, delicatesse, melange) with a freedom that did not please scholars at all, since English is entirely equal to the expression he sought. He wrestled with the big commonplace world of the United States, and managed, after his own strange fashion, to express its grandeur. But even the United States was too restricted a theme for him. He tried to express the human being inside and out, body, brains, and soul, and in the ardor of his composition found the shackles of rhyme and rhythm, sometimes of reason also, too strict for what he wished to say. Hence the quaint form of his poetic speech, the lists of qualities and attributes, organs and functions, tools, instruments, and things used in the trades and other occupations of man.

He was orbic, and wished to embrace everything in the mirror of his verse like those spheres of polished metal that stand on lawns. Like them he succeeded in being a curiosity while he lived rather than the mirror which people are in the habit of consulting. His very power oppressed him. Ill-digested and shapeless as his work is compared to the poetry of the great bards of the past, Whitman resembled one of those poets of medieval Ireland who were crammed with a large amount of ill-assorted knowledge and turgid in rhetoric, but filled with the truest poetic flame and really appreciated only by the extremely naive on the one hand, and on the other by people of the widest sympathies, the deepest knowledge, and the keenest critical faculty. We may liken him to such poets as were found in Ireland by Edmund Spenser in the sixteenth century, whose songs, when duly translated for him into English, "compelled his admiration."

. . . It is impossible to forecast what Whitman's place in American literature is going to be. For one thing he represents, as no college graduate and scholarly man has hitherto, the great bulk of the Nation educated in common schools. Yet hitherto he has been the scholar's delight, and the people will have none of him, unless it be a jewel from "Drum-Taps," or a rhapsody entirely free from physiological theories like that beginning "Out of the cradle endlessly rocking," a threnody on a forsaken mocking bird, which ranks with the greatest productions of genius in English.

At any rate, posterity is not going to judge him as harshly as some of the virtuous of today have done, for how can the men of the future fail to be won over by a man who believes so rapturously in the essential goodness of all created things—even of that pit, the soul of man? In one of the notes which run as the subsidiary stream in small type at the foot of the pages of "Two Rivulets," the poet, apparently staggered at the attempt to understand himself or his real object, hazards this opinion (it is in the preface:) "Probably, indeed, the whole of these varied songs, and all my writings, both volumes, only ring changes in some sort, on the ejaculation: How vast, how eligible, how joyful, how real, is a Human Being, himself or herself!"

Barrett Wendell on Whitman

... The vagaries of Walt Whitman, ... are as far from literary conscience as the animals which he somewhere celebrates are from unhappiness or respectability. Whitman's style, then, is as little characteristic of America as his temper is of traditional American democracy. One can see why the decadent taste of modern Europe has welcomed him so much more ardently than he has ever been welcomed at home; in temper and in style he was an exotic member of that sterile brotherhood which eagerly greeted him abroad. In America his oddities were more eccentric than they would have been anywhere else.

On the other hand, there is an aspect in which he seems not only native but even promising. During the years when his observation was keenest, and his temper most alert, he lived in the environment from which our future America seems most likely to spring. He was born and grew up, he worked and lived, where on either side of the East River the old American towns of New York and Brooklyn were developing into the metropolis which is still too young to possess ripe traditions. In full maturity he devoted himself to army nursing,—the least picturesque or glorious, and the most humanely heroic, service which he could have rendered his country during its agony of civil war. In that Civil War the elder America perished; the new America which then arose is not yet mature enough for artistic record. Whitman's

From *A Literary History of America,* by Barrett Wendell, New York: Charles Scribner's Sons, 1901, pp. 477–479.

earthly experience, then, came throughout in chaotic times, when our past had faded and our future had not yet sprung into being. Bewildering confusion, fused by the accident of his lifetime into the seeming unity of a momentary whole, was the only aspect of human existence which could be afforded him by the native country which he so truly loved. For want of other surroundings he was content to seek the meaning of life amid New York slums and dingy suburban country, in the crossing of Brooklyn Ferry, or in the hospitals which strove to alleviate the drums and tramplings of civil war. His lifelong eagerness to find in life the stuff of which poetry is made has brought him, after all, the reward he would most have cared for. In one aspect he is thoroughly American. The spirit of his work is that of world-old anarchy; its form has all the perverse oddity of world-old abortive decadence; but the substance of which his poems are made—their imagery as distinguished from their form or their spirit—comes wholly from our native country.

In this aspect, then, though probably in no other, he may, after all, throw light on the future of literature in America. As has been said before, "He is uncouth, inarticulate, whatever you please that is least orthodox; yet, after all, he can make you feel for the moment how even the ferry-boats plying from New York to Brooklyn are fragments of God's eternities. Those of us who love the past are far from sharing his confidence in the future. Surely, however, that is no reason for denying the miracle that he has wrought by idealising the East River. The man who has done this is the only one who points out the stuff of which perhaps the new American literature of the future may in time be made."

Alfred North Whitehead on Whitman

". . . Suppose our American culture were wiped out: whom have we produced so far who would stand as a lasting contribution to the world?"

"Walt Whitman."

"Not Emerson?"

"I read Emerson a good deal when I was younger, but if my good neighbours, the Forbeses, will pardon me for saying so, (they are grandsons of Emerson) he was not so original. But Whitman brought something into poetry which was never there before. Much of what he says is so new that he even had to invent a form for saying it. Whitman seems to me to have been one of the few very great poets that have ever lived. He can stand easily beside the really great European poets. . . ."

". . . Whitman's poems *represent* his world and himself much more satisfactorily than Tennyson's do his. In the past a few poets have both formed and represented, each in the highest degree; but in modern times what controlling, organizing, selecting poet has created a world with as much in it as Whitman's, a world that so plainly *is* the world? Of all modern poets he has, quantitatively speaking, 'the most comprehensive soul'—and,

From *Dialogues of Alfred North Whitehead*, Boston: Little Brown, 1954 (reprinted in A Mentor Book, 1956, 1964). By permission of Little, Brown and Co.

qualitatively, a most comprehensive and comprehending one, with charities and concessions and qualifications that are rare in any time. . . ."

". . . The artist," said Whitehead, "has, and must have, a continuous flow of fresh aesthetic experiences. These he translates into an art-form, and it is through these works that his experience passes into the lives of others." He let it go at that, but he knew, and I knew, that what he had said meant more than met the ear.

"So morals have nothing to do with good poetry?"

"Was Byron 'moral'?" he inquired, smilingly.

Of a sudden he had me on his side:

"That is one thing which ails so many of our American nineteenth-century poets. They are entirely too 'correct'—in their printed sentiments at least. Reading them now, one finds himself thinking: 'You didn't really believe that. It's not possible that you didn't know better. Only you didn't dare say so!' A sample in prose of that timidity is the feeble 'moral' which Hawthorne ventures at the end of *The Scarlet Letter!* 'Be true! Show freely to the world, if not your worst, yet some trait whereby the worst can be inferred!' Even as a boy, reading that, I knew it was evasive. 'If you can't be true, be as true as you can!' "

"The one of your poets who escapes all that," said Mrs. Whitehead, "is Whitman. And American poetry has never elsewhere reached such heights as in his elegy for President Lincoln."

Some Lines from Whitman

. . . To show Whitman for what he is one does not need to praise or explain or argue, one needs simply to quote. He himself said, "I and mine do not convince by arguments, similes, rhymes,/ We convince by our presence." Even a few of his phrases are enough to show us that Whitman was no sweeping rhetorician, but a poet of the greatest and oddest delicacy and originality and sensitivity, so far as words are concerned. This is, after all, the poet who said, "Blind loving wrestling touch, sheath'd hooded sharp-tooth'd touch"; who said, "Smartly attired, countenance smiling, form upright, death under the breast-bones, hell under the skull-bones"; who said, "Agonies are one of my changes of garments"; who saw grass as the "flag of my disposition," saw "the sharp-peak'd farmhouse, with its scallop'd scum and slender shoots from the gutters," heard a plane's "wild ascending lisp," and saw and heard how at the amputation "what is removed drops horribly in a pail." This is the poet for whom the sea was "howler and scooper of storms," reaching out to us with "crooked inviting fingers"; who went "leaping chasms with a pike-pointed staff, clinging to topples of brittle and blue"; who, a runaway slave, saw how "my gore dribs, thinn'd with the ooze of my skin"; who went "lithographing Kronos . . . buying drafts of Osiris"; who stared out at the "little plentiful mannikins skipping around in collars and tail'd coat,/ I am aware who they are, (they are posi-

From *Poetry and the Age*, by Randall Jarrell, New York: Alfred A. Knopf, Inc., 1953. Used by permission.

tively not worms or fleas)." For he is, at his best, beautifully witty: he says gravely, "I find I incorporate gneiss, coals, long-threaded moss, fruits, grain, esculent roots,/And am stucco'd with quadrupeds and birds all over"; and of these quadrupeds and birds "not one is respectable or unhappy over the whole earth." He calls advice: "Unscrew the locks from the doors! Unscrew the doors from their jambs!" He publishes the results of research: "Having pried through the strata, analyz'd to a hair, counsel'd with doctors and calculated close,/ I find no sweeter fat than sticks to my own bones." Everybody remembers how he told the Muse to "cross out please those immensely over-paid accounts,/ That matter of Troy and Achilles' wrath, and Aeneas', Odysseus' wanderings," but his account of the arrival of the "illustrious emigré" here in the New World is even better: "Bluff'd not a bit by drainpipe, gasometer, artificial fertilizers,/ Smiling and pleas'd with palpable intent to stay,/ She's here, install'd amid the kitchenware." Or he sees, like another Breughel, "the mechanic's wife with the babe at her nipple interceding for every person born,/ Three scythes at harvest whizzing in a row from three lusty angels with shirts bagg'd out at their waists,/ The snag-toothed hostler with red hair redeeming sins past and to come"—the passage has enough wit not only (in Johnson's phrase) to keep it sweet, but enough to make it believable. . . .

Symbols of Dimension

...For a generation after the War of 1812 American patriotism developed in the direction of a cosmic philosophy of social evolution. Or it might more accurately be called a religion based on the faith that the Creator had selected the North American continent for the scene of the culminating civilization in world history. In 1839 an editorial in the *Democratic Review* (a magazine to which Whitman contributed a few years later) declared: "It would, perhaps, not be too extravagant to say that the poetical resources of our country are boundless. Nature has here granted everything to genius which can excite, exalt, enlarge, and ennoble its powers. Nothing is narrow, nothing is confined. All is height, all is expansion.... Our history, too, is poetical."

Whitman's exploitation of size, therefore, was not the result merely of the fact that his own body was large and strong, for spatial dimensions symbolized Americans' conceit of themselves and their cultural and moral aspirations, and Whitman's consciousness was saturated by the national consciousness. "Here at last is something in the doings of man that corresponds with the broadcast doings of the day and night.... Here are the roughs and beards and space and ruggedness and nonchalance that the soul loves." This wide, fertile, seemingly inexhaustible continent invited "a corresponding largeness and generosity of the spirit

From Introduction to *Walt Whitman's Poems*, edited by Gay Wilson Allen and Charles T. Davis, New York University Press, 1955. Used by permission.

of the citizen." It called for amplitude in the poet, too. "The greatest poet hardly knows pettiness or triviality. If he breathes into anything that was before thought small it dilates with the grandeur and life of the universe."

There can be no doubt that Whitman's personal life was profoundly influenced by this national dream of expansion and development, but the point is that he expressed in his poems not the character and personality actually his in everyday life so much as the vision of physical and spiritual power he shared with the nation. The folk mind created its mythical heroes of supernatural strength: Paul Bunyan, Davy Crockett, John Henry, Mike Fink—demigods of untamed forests and rivers and a raw civilization. On the same scale Walt Whitman created his mythical poet, whom he personified in himself. In writing his 1855 Preface he knew that his poet was a myth, though a very intoxicating one, and in writing his best early poems he drew strength from the potency of the myth. But in a short time he began to confuse the myth with his deliberately cultivated personality, and in subsequent attempts to elucidate his *Leaves of Grass* he was as likely to obscure as to clarify his purpose in writing his poems— and still more to obscure what he had actually accomplished in a given poem.

Despite many discouragements, Whitman lived a long and productive life, and his artistic motives varied from time to time. Sometimes he wrote, as he confessed in 1876, to express his "irrepressible yearning" for love, to appease his "never-satisfied appetite for sympathy." Indeed, such psychological motives may have nurtured his poetic faculties, but in his greatest lyrics, such as "Out of the Cradle" and "When Lilacs Last," he created an artistic form as a vehicle for the mythopoeic experience of the race. Here his themes were birth, death, and resurrection—the basic themes of nearly all the world's greatest religious and cultural myths—for which he found appropriate symbolic imagery and rhythms. In these masterpieces the poet transcended his personality, and even the national consciousness.

Three motives, then, competed in Whitman's mind when he

attempted to exercise his poetic faculties: the desire to celebrate himself and exploit his own real or imagined personality, the ambition to celebrate his nation and give artistic embodiment to its highest aspirations and an intuition of the meaning of the great life mysteries: birth, death, and the hope of resurrection. . . .

Whitman's Innovations

... What [Whitman] is saying there [in his prefaces] is that he is hewing out his own kind of craftsmanship in order to contain his own particular kind of personal feeling. This is a moment of time; this individual confronts this time and it is possible, if he cultivates the proper kind of awareness, if he trains his sensibilty, if he poses it in the proper way, to achieve a cosmic vision which relates all time and all space to the individual. Only by being true to one's own self can one ever come to terms with outside reality....

In what respects, then, was Whitman a rebel, what did he rebel against, and how fruitful was his rebellion? It seems to me that his main objective was to come to terms with the nature of identity, the nature of personality; to explore new ways of relating a full relish of personal identity with a full savouring of life existing in the teeming world around him, whether of other people or of nature. What he rebelled against was the implication of the Victorian assumption that the poet must surrender either to elegy or to didacticism, the assumption that these are incompatible alternatives and, further, that directing of sensibility into pre-determined channels was the only way of writing a poem. What he won for the future in this rebellion was a new way of relating loneliness to love, the great perennial problem of modern litera-

From "Walt Whitman as Innovator," by David Daiches, in *The Young Rebel in American Literature: Seven Lectures*, edited by Carl Bode, London: Heinemann, 1959. Used by permission.

ture. It was a way that involved a consciousness of the *otherness* of other people, a new kind of dependence on the consciousness closely akin to the stream-of-consciousness method in modern fiction, and a mode of poetical utterance which depended for its structure on a mosaic of ideas and impressions rather than on set forms.

And where does that take us? Precisely to the heart of the one great modern poet who has ignored and undervalued Whitman— Mr. Eliot himself. Whitman's Brooklyn is not unlike Eliot's London. Both poets were similarly aware of the rhythms of modern life. Both used the mosaic of ideas, the special kind of poetic dialectic achieved by patterning fragments of the civilization you are presenting into a kind of eloquent and symbolic jigsaw. Whitman did that in his own way before Eliot did and it seems to me that no American poet, whether he accepts or rejects Whitman, can fail to have profited. It sometimes seems to me that the tragedy of Whitman is exactly the same as the tragedy of my native Scottish poet, Robert Burns. Both were admired for the wrong reasons and the people who imitated them most directly were the worst poets. The so-called Whitmanians of the twentieth century were those who cultivated a shrill patriotic rhetoric, but that is not the true Whitman idiom. I myself believe that the mosaic of ideas in Eliot, the stream of consciousness in the modern novel, and all those extraordinarily subtle devices through which the modern novelist and poet have tried to explore ways in which an individual sensibility can be modulated into an inclusive consciousness, are in the tradition of Whitman. How to escape the prison of the self and cultivate simultaneously self-consciousness and sympathy, using a sense of self-identity as a means of projecting oneself into the identity of others—that, I think, is Whitman's most valuable legacy to modern literature."

Chronology

1819	Born May 31 at West Hills, near Huntington, Long Island, New York.
1823	Whitman family moved to Brooklyn.
1830(?)–34	Learning printing trade.
1835	Printer in New York City until great fire August 12.
1836–38	Summer of 1836 begins teaching school at East Norwich, Long Island; by winter of 1837–38 had taught at Hempstead, Babylon, Long Swamp, and Smithtown.
1838–39	Edits newspaper, the *Long Islander*, at Huntington, about twelve months; works on newspaper at Jamaica, the *Long Island Democrat*; contributes "Sun-Down Papers from the Desk of a Schoolmaster" while teaching school at Little Bay Side (near Jamaica).
1840–41	In late summer and autumn 1840 electioneers for Van Buren; then teaches school at Trimming Square, Woodbury, Dix Hills, and Whitestone.
1841	Goes to New York City in May as printer in *New World* office and begins writing for the *Democratic Review*.
1842	For about two months in spring edits a daily newspaper, the *New York Aurora;* edits the *Evening Tattler* for a few months.

1845–46   In August returns to Brooklyn, writes for *Long Island Star* from September, 1845, until March, 1846.

1846–48   From March, 1846, until late January, 1848, editor of *Brooklyn Daily Eagle;* in February, 1848, trip to New Orleans via railroad, stagecoach, and steamboat; employed on *New Orleans Crescent* from March 5 to May 25; returns by boat via Mississippi, Great Lakes and Hudson River.

1848–49   From September 9, 1848, to September 11, 1849, editor of *Brooklyn Freeman,* a "Free Soil" newspaper.

1850–54   Operates printing office and stationery store; does free-lance writing for newspapers; mainly a building contractor and real estate speculator.

1855   Early July, *Leaves of Grass* printed by Rome Brothers in Brooklyn; father dies July 11.

1856   Second edition of *Leaves of Grass* printed in summer. "The Eighteenth Presidency" written; copies survive only in proof sheets.

1857–59   From spring of 1857 to mid-summer of 1859, editor of *Brooklyn Times.*

1860   March, 1860, in Boston to see new edition of *Leaves of Grass* through the press, published in May by Thayer & Eldridge; June 16, Japanese "ambassadors" parade on Broadway and Whitman writes "The Errand-Bearers" ("A Broadway Pageant"); frequents Pfaff's restaurant.

1861   April 12, Fort Sumter fired upon by Confederate batteries—beginning of Civil War.

1862   In December goes to Fredericksburg, scene of recent battle in which George Whitman was wounded, stays in camp about two weeks; remained in Washington, D.C., working part-time in Paymaster's Office, visiting soldiers in hospitals.

1863–64   Hospital visits in Washington continue until mid-
               June, 1864; returns to Brooklyn because of ill-
               health.

1865   January 24, appointed clerk in Department of In-
               terior and returns to Washington.
               March 4, second inauguration of President Lincoln
               witnessed by Whitman. While he is visiting his
               family in Brooklyn, Lincoln assassinated April 14.
               George recently released from Confederate prison.
               May, *Drum-Taps* printed.
               Discharged from position in Department of Inter-
               ior by Secretary James Harlan on June 30; re-
               employed next day in Attorney General's Office.
               Sequel to Drum-Taps, containing "When Lilacs
               Last in the Door-Yard Bloom'd," printed in Sep-
               tember.

1866   In January, William D. O'Connor's *Good Gray
               Poet* published by Bunce & Harrington, New York
               City.

1867   Publication of first biography of Whitman, John
               Burroughs' *Notes on Walt Whitman as Poet and
               Person;* William Rossetti publishes article on Whit-
               man's poetry in *London Chronicle*, July 6.
               Fourth edition of *Leaves of Grass* printed.
               "Democracy" (part of *Democratic Vistas*) in De-
               cember *Galaxy*.

1868   William Rossetti's selected English edition (slightly
               expurgated) of *Poems of Walt Whitman;* wider
               recognition in England.
               "Personalism" (part of *Democratic Vistas*) in May
               Galaxy.
               Second issue of fourth edition of *Leaves of Grass*
               with *Drum-Taps* and *Sequel* added.

1870   July 15, beginning of Franco-Prussian War; Whit-
               man very depressed for personal reasons.

1871 Fifth edition of *Leaves of Grass*, containing "Passage to India."

September 3, Mrs. Anne Gilchrist's first love letter to Whitman.

1872 "As a Strong Bird on Pinions Free" read at Dartmouth College Commencement, June 26.

"After All Not to Create Only" ("Song of the Exposition") read at National Industrial Exposition in New York, September 7.

Quarrel with O'Connor and end of friendship.

Swinburne's attack in "Under the Microscope."

1873 Paralytic stroke night of January 23, 1873.

Death of poet's mother, May 23, in Camden, New Jersey; unable to work, has to live with brother George in Camden.

1874 Publication of "Song of the Redwood-Tree" and "Prayer of Columbus."

1875 Centennial Edition of *Leaves of Grass* and *Two Rivulets* printed (dated 1876).

1876 Controversy in British and American press over America's neglect of Whitman.

In spring, begins visits to Stafford Farm.

In September, Mrs. Gilchrist arrives in United States.

1879 First lecture on Lincoln, April 14, Philadelphia.

Trip to West (Colorado), September, 1879, to January, 1880.

1880 Summer, trip to London, Ontario, to visit Dr. R. M. Bucke.

1881 Lincoln lecture given in Boston in April.

James R. Osgood, Boston, publishes *Leaves of Grass*.

1882 In spring, District Attorney threatens prosecution and Osgood gives up *Leaves of Grass;* publication resumed by Rees Welsh & Co., of Philadelphia, which also publishes *Specimen Days and Collect.* Both books transferred to David McKay, Philadelphia.

1883 Dr. R. M. Bucke publishes *Walt Whitman*, a biography on which the poet had assisted.

1884 Buys house on Mickle Street in Camden, New Jersey.

1887 Lincoln lecture given in New York.
      Sculptured by Sidney Morse; painted by Herbert Gilchrist, J. W. Alexander, and Thomas Eakins.

1888 Horace Traubel raises funds for doctors and nurses.
      November Boughs printed.

1889 Birthday dinner, proceedings published as *Camden's Compliments.*

1890 Letter from John Addington Symonds provokes poet to claim six unacknowledged children.

1891 *Good-Bye My Fancy* printed.

1892 Ninth edition of *Leaves of Grass.*
      Death of poet March 26; buried in Harleigh Cemetery, Camden, New Jersey.

Bibliographical Check List

EDITIONS

Leaves of Grass. [First edition.] Brooklyn, N.Y. 1855. 95 pp.

Leaves of Grass. [Second edition.] Brooklyn, N.Y. 1856. 384 pp.

Leaves of Grass. [Third edition.] Boston: Thayer and Eldridge, 1860–61. 456 pp.

Drum-Taps. New York. 1865. 72 pp. *Drum-Taps and Sequel.* 1865. 72 + 24 pp.

Leaves of Grass. [Fourth edition.] New York. 1867. 338 pp.

Democratic Vistas. Washington, D.C. 1871. 84 pp.

Leaves of Grass. [Fifth edition.] Washington, D.C. 1871. 384 pp. *With Passage to India.* 1872. 120 pp.

Leaves of Grass. [Sixth edition.] Camden, N.J. 1876. (Vol. I of Author's Edition of *Complete Works.*)

Two Rivulets. Including *Democratic Vistas, Centennial Songs,* and *Passage to India.* Camden, N.J. 1876. (Vol. II of Author's Edition of *Complete Works.*)

Leaves of Grass. [Seventh edition.] Boston: James R. Osgood and Co., 1881–82. 382 pp. (Reprinted in Philadelphia by Rees Welsh and Co. in 1882 and by David McKay.)

Specimen Days and Collect. Philadelphia: Rees Welsh and Co., 1882–83. 374 pp. (Volume of *Complete Works* as companion to *Leaves of Grass* reprinted by Rees Welsh and Co. in 1882.)

November Boughs. Philadelphia: David McKay, 1888. 140 pp.

Complete Poems and Prose of Walt Whitman, 1855–1888.

[Eighth edition of poems, third of *Complete Works*.] Philadelphia: published by the author, 1888. 382 + 374 pp.

Leaves of Grass, with *Sands at Seventy* and *A Backward Glance O'er Travel'd Roads*. [Eighth separate edition of poems.] Philadelphia, 1889. 404 + 18 pp.

Good-Bye, My Fancy. [Second Annex to *Leaves of Grass;* first was "Sands at Seventy" in eighth edition of poems.] Philadelphia: David McKay, 1891. 66 pp.

Leaves of Grass. [Ninth edition.] Philadelphia: David McKay, 1891–1892. 438 pp. (Also bound as Vol. I of the fourth edition of *Complete Works* to p. 383, reprint of 1881 edition; new poems annexed pp. 383–422.)

Complete Prose Works. Philadelphia: David McKay, 1892. 522 pp. (Also bound as Vol. II of *Complete Works;* later redated 1894 and 1897.)

Leaves of Grass. [Tenth edition.] Boston: Small, Maynard and Co., 1897. 455 pp. (Includes posthumous poems, "Old Age Echoes.")

The Complete Writings of Walt Whitman. Issued under the editorial supervision of the Literary Executors. New York and London: G. P. Putnam's Sons, 1902. 10 vols.

The Collected Writings of Walt Whitman,
under General Editorship of Gay Wilson Allen and Sculley Bradley, in process of publication by New York University Press. Published to date: *The Correspondence*, edited by Edwin Haviland Miller. Vols. I–V (complete). 1961–69. *The Early Poems and the Fiction*, edited by Thomas L. Brasher, 1963.
Prose Works 1892, edited by Floyd Stovall: Vol. I: *Specimen Days*, 1963; Vol. II: *Collect and Other Prose*, 1964. *Leaves of Grass: Comprehensive Reader's Edition*, edited by Harold W. Blodgett and Sculley Bradley, 1965.
[Future volumes will include a Variorum *Leaves of Grass*, Diaries and Notebooks, Journalistic Writings, and a Bibliography.]

UNCOLLECTED WRITINGS (In Order of Publication)

Calamus. A Series of Letters Written during the Years 1868–1880. By Walt Whitman to a Young Friend (Peter Doyle). Ed. by Richard Maurice Bucke, M.D. Boston: Laurens Maynard. 1897. viii, 172 pp.

The Wound Dresser. A Series of Letters Written from the Hospitals in Washington during the War of the Rebellion by Walt Whitman. Ed. by Richard Maurice Bucke, M.D. Boston: Small, Maynard and Co. 1898. viii, 201 pp.

Notes and Fragments. Ed. by Dr. Richard Maurice Bucke. (Printed for private distribution.) London, Ontario, Canada. 1899. 211 pp.

Letters Written by Walt Whitman to His Mother From 1866 to 1872. Ed. by Thomas B. Harned. New York and London: G. P. Putnam's Sons. 1902. 132 pp.

Walt Whitman's Diary in Canada. Ed. by William Sloane Kennedy. Boston: Small, Maynard and Co. 1904. 73 pp.

An American Primer. [Notes on language and style.] Ed. by Horace Traubel. Boston: Small, Maynard and Co. 1904. 35 pp.

The Letters of Anne Gilchrist and Walt Whitman. Ed. by Thomas B. Harned. New York: Doubleday, Page and Co. 1918. 242 pp.

The Gathering of the Forces. [Mainly editorials in the Brooklyn *Daily Eagle* in 1846–47.] Ed. by Cleveland Rodgers and John Black. New York and London: G. P. Putnam's Sons. 1920. 2 vols.

The Uncollected Poetry and Prose of Walt Whitman. [Poems published before *Leaves of Grass* and prose from stories, editorials, reviews, diaries, manuscript notes, etc.] Ed. by Emory Holloway. New York: Doubleday, Page and Co. 1921. 2 vols.

Pictures. An Unpublished Poem by Walt Whitman. Ed. by Emory Holloway. New York: The June House. 1927. London: Faber and Gwyer. 1927. 37 pp.

The Half-Breed and Other Stories. Ed. by Thomas Ollive Mabbott. New York: Columbia University Press. 1927. 129 pp.

Walt Whitman's Workshop. [Speeches, unpublished prefaces, and other fragments in Library of Congress.] Ed. by Clifton J. Furness. Cambridge: Harvard University Press. 1928. 265 pp.

The Eighteenth Presidency. Voice of Walt Whitman to Each Young Man in the Nation, North, South, East and West. Note by Jean Catel. Montpellier, France, Causse, Graille and Castelnau. 1928. 31 pp. (See 1956 edition below.)

A Child's Reminiscence. Ed. by Thomas O. Mabbott and Rollo G. Silver. [First published text and self-written review of the poem "Out of the Cradle . . ."] Seattle: University of Washington Book Store. 1930. 44 pp.

I Sit and Look Out. Editorials from the Brooklyn *Daily Times.* Ed. by Emory Holloway and Vernolian Schwarz. New York: Columbia University Press. 1932. 248 pp.

Walt Whitman and the Civil War. A Collection of Original Articles and Manuscripts. Ed. by Charles I. Glicksberg. Philadelphia: University of Pennsylvania Press. 1933. 201 pp.

New York Dissected. [Newspaper articles of the 1850's] Ed. by Emory Holloway and Ralph Adimari. New York: Rufus Rockwell Wilson. 1936. 257 pp.

Walt Whitman's Backward Glances . . . [Origin and early versions of the essay.] Ed. by Sculley Bradley and John A. Stevenson. Philadelphia: University of Pennsylvania Press. 1947. 51 pp.

Faint Clews & Indirections: Manuscripts of Walt Whitman and His Family. Ed. by Clarence Gohdes and Rollo G. Silver. Durham: Duke University Press. 1949. 250 pp.

Walt Whitman Looks at the Schools. [Editorials and articles of the 1840's. Ed. by Florence Bernstein Freedman. New York: King's Crown Press. 1950. 278 pp.

Walt Whitman of the New York Aurora: Editor at Twenty-

Two. Ed. by Joseph Jay Rubin and Charles H. Brown. State College, Pennsylvania: Bald Eagle Press. 1950. 148 pp.

Whitman's Manuscripts: Leaves of Grass (1860): A Parallel Text. Ed. by Fredson Bowers. Chicago: University of Chicago Press. 1955. lxxiv, 264 pp.

The Eighteenth Presidency: A Critical Text. Ed. by Edward F. Grier. Lawrence: University of Kansas Press. 1956. 47 pp.

An 1855–56 Notebook: Toward the Second Edition of Leaves of Grass. Introduction and Notes by Harold W. Blodgett. With Foreword by Charles E. Feinberg. Additional Notes by William White. Carbondale: Southern Illinois University Press. 1959. 41 pp.

The Early Poems and the Fiction. Ed. by Thomas L. Brasher. New York: The New York University Press. 1963.

REPRINTS AND SELECTIONS

Walt Whitman's Leaves of Grass: The First (1855) Edition. Ed. with an Introduction by Malcolm Cowley. New York: Viking. 1959. 145 pp.

Leaves of Grass. Facsimile Edition of the 1860 Text. With an Introduction by Roy Harvey Pearce. Cornell University Press. 1961. 467 pp.

Walt Whitman's Blue Book: The 1860–61 Leaves of Grass. Containing His Manuscript Additions and Revisions. Ed. by Arthur Golden. Vol. I: Facsimile. Vol. II: Textual Analysis. New York Public Library. 1968.

Walt Whitman's Poems. Selections with Critical Aids. Ed. by Gay Wilson Allen and Charles T. Davis. New York University Press. 1955. 1968.

Whitman. The Laurel Poetry Series. Selected, with an Introduction and Notes, by Leslie A. Fiedler. New York: Dell. 1959.

BOOKS ABOUT WHITMAN

Allen, Gay Wilson. *The Solitary Singer: A Critical Biography of*

Walt Whitman. New York: Macmillan. 1955. Grove. 1959.
Rev. Ed.: New York University Press. 1967. 616 pp.
————. *Walt Whitman as Man, Poet, and Legend*. With a Check
   List of Whitman Publications 1945–1960, by Evie Allison
   Allen. Southern Illinois University Press. 1961. 260 pp.
Asselineau, Roger. *L'Evolution de Walt Whitman: Après la
   première édition des Feuilles d'herbe*. Paris: Didier. 1954.
   567 pp. *The Evolution of Walt Whitman: The Creation
   of a Poet*. Harvard University Press. 1960. 376 pp. *The Evo-
   lution of Walt Whitman: The Creation of a Book*. Harvard
   University Press. 1962. 392 pp.
Balzagette, Léon. *Le "Poème-Evangile" de Walt Whitman*.
   Paris: Mercure de France. 1921. 357 pp.
Beaver, Joseph. *Walt Whitman, Poet of Science*. New York:
   King's Crown Press. 1951. 178 pp.
Binns, Henry B. *A Life of Walt Whitman*. London: Methuen.
   1905. xxviii, 369 pp.
Blodgett, Harold W. *Walt Whitman in England*. Cornell Uni-
   versity Press. 1934. 244 pp.
Bucke, Richard M. *Walt Whitman*. Philadelphia: David McKay.
   1883. 236 pp.
Burroughs, John. *Notes on Walt Whitman, as Poet and Person*.
   New York: American News Co. 1867. 108 pp. New York:
   J. S. Redfield. 1871. 126 pp.
Canby, Henry S. *Walt Whitman, an American: A Study in Bi-
   ography*. Boston: Houghton Mifflin Co. 1943. 381 pp.
Carpenter, Edward. *Days with Walt Whitman*. New York:
   Macmillan. 1906. 187 pp.
Catel, Jean. *Walt Whitman: La Naissance du Poète*. Paris: Rieder.
   1929. 483 pp.
Chukovskii, Kornei. *Moii Uhtmen* [My Whitman, long bio-
   graphical-critical Introduction, selected translations, biblio-
   graphical notes]. Mosco: State Publishing Co. "Progress."
   1966. 271 pp.
De Selincourt, Basil. *Walt Whitman: A Critical Study*. London:
   M. Secker. 1914. 250 pp.

Dutton, Geoffrey. *Whitman*. Edinburgh: Oliver and Boyd Ltd. 1961. New York: Grove Press. 1961.

Faner, Robert D. *Walt Whitman & Opera*. University of Pennsylvania Press. 1951. 249 pp.

Holloway, Emory. *Whitman: An Interpretation in Narrative*. New York: Alfred A. Knopf. 1926. 330 pp.

Kennedy, William Sloane. *The Fight of a Book for the World*. West Yarmouth, Mass.: Stonecroft Press. 1926. 304 pp.

──────. *Reminiscences of Walt Whitman*. London: A. Gardner. 1896. 190 pp.

Miller, James E., Jr. *A Critical Guide to Leaves of Grass*. University of Chicago Press. 1957. 268 pp.

──────. Shapiro, Karl, and Slote, Bernice. *Start with the Sun: Studies in Cosmic Poetry*. University of Nebraska Press. 1960.

O'Connor, William D. *The Good Gray Poet: A Vindication*. New York: Bunce & Harrington. 1866. 46 pp.

Perry, Bliss. *Walt Whitman: His Life and Work*. Boston: Houghton Mifflin and Co. 1906. 318 pp.

Schyberg, Frederik. *Walt Whitman*. København: Gyldendal. 1933. 349 pp. Translated into English by Evie Allison Allen. Columbia University Press. 1951. 387 pp.

Symonds, John A. *Walt Whitman: A Study*. London: J. C. Nimmo. 1893. xxxv, 160 pp.

Traubel, Horace, ed. *In Re Walt Whitman*. Ed. by Literary Executors. Philadelphia: David McKay. 1893. 452 pp.

──────. *With Walt Whitman in Camden*. Vol. I, Boston: Small Maynard. 1906. Vol. II, New York: D. Appleton and Co. 1908. Vol. III, New York: Mitchell Kennerly. 1904. Vol. IV, Philadelphia: University of Pennsylvania Press. 1953. Vol. IV, second issue, Carbondale, Illinois: Southern Illinois University Press. 1959. [Other volumes in process of being edited.]

The Walt Whitman Review, Wayne State University Press, Detroit, Michigan, prints scholarly and critical articles on Whitman and lists current publications.

Acknowledgments

Walt Whitman House, Camden, N.J.
Brooklyn Museum
The Macmillan Co., N.Y.
Stokes Collection, New York Public Library
Duke University Library
Eno Collection, New York Public Library
Museum of the City of New York
Oscar Lion Collection, New York Public Library
Charles E. Feinberg
C. N. Elliot
Harper's Weekly
Chief Signal Officer, National Archives
Whitman Collection, Manuscript Division, Library of Congress
Edward Naumberg, Jr.
Milton I. D. Einstein
Dr. William Reeder
Frank Leslie's Weekly
Pennsylvania Academy of Fine Arts
The Metropolitan Museum of Art, New York
University of Pennsylvania Library

Index

Gay Wilson Allen received his B.A. and M.A. degrees from Duke University (1926, 1929), and his Ph.D. from the University of Wisconsin (1934). He is currently professor of English at New York University. Professor Allen is best-known for his literary biographies, among which are The Solitary Singer: A Critical Biography of Walt Whitman *(1955), and* William James: A Biography *(1967). He is general editor (with Sculley Bradley) of* The Collected Writings of Walt Whitman.

The manuscript was edited by Ralph R. Busick. The book was designed by Edgar Frank. The type face for the text is Janson's Old Style and was designed by Nicholas Kis in the 17th Century. The display faces include Allegro designed by Hans Bohn in the 20th century and Weiss Series 1 designed by E. R. Weiss for Bauer in 1931.

manufactured in the United States of America.